RANGERS

The Official Illustrated History

Stephen Halliday

Foreword by
Graeme Souness

ARTHUR BARKER
A division of Weidenfeld and Nicolson London

To Dad, Mum and Ange – Thank You

Acknowledgements

The author would like to thank the following people for their invaluable help without which the production of this book would have been impossible. David Mason for his assistance in supplying old and rare photographs from the Ibrox archives and for reading the text prior to publication; Alan Ewing for taking some of the photographs; Charles Freeland for his constant help and encouragement through my career; Robert McElroy for checking the statistics; the *Glasgow Herald, Evening Times, Hulton-Deutsch Collection and Syndication International* for permission to reproduce the black-and-white photographs; All-Sport and Sportapic for permission to reproduce the colour photographs; my family for their inspiration and, last but not least, my wife Ange without whom the deadlines would never have been met.

Front endpapers: The Ibrox faithful.
Opposite title page: At the threshold.

Published in Great Britain by
George Weidenfeld & Nicolson Limited
91 Clapham High Street, London SW4 7TA

ISBN 0 213 16924 X

Printed in Great Britain by
Butler & Tanner Ltd, Frome and London

Contents

Foreword by Graeme Souness   9

Introduction   11

1   In the Beginning   13
2   The Wee Blue Devil and Other
    Heroes   25
3   End of an Era   43
4   John Lawrence and Scot Symon   53
5   The Swinging Sixties   65
6   Triumph in Europe   78
7   Jock and John   99
8   Rangers are Born Again   122

Rangers Records   147

GRAEME SOUNESS   On and off the field, the sophisticated superstar has changed Rangers.
His fierce determination and ambition should see the club in good stead for the challenge ahead.

Foreword
by Graeme Souness

It is a privilege for me to be able to write the foreword to this book, and a privilege to occupy the manager's chair at Ibrox in such exciting times for Rangers Football Club. I never dreamed that I would hold such a position at this stage of my footballing career and even now, over three years since taking over at Ibrox, I have to pinch myself sometimes to make sure it's all not simply a dream.

All of us at Ibrox must always remember what being a part of Rangers Football Club means – that is something I insist upon and anyone who forgets will get no sympathy from me. I have the best job in British football and my players are playing for the biggest club in Britain and must perform to the standards expected of Rangers players. Just a quick glance through the pages of this book will show anyone what we must live up to, maintain and, if at all possible, improve upon. The great players, famous games and astonishing honours list of this club make awesome reading.

From my own personal recollections, the sight of Jim Baxter gracing the pitch at Ibrox was something special that has never been surpassed. Many of the people coming to Ibrox to support us today will talk of men like Willie Waddell and Willie Thornton with the same reverence, while the greatness of players from even further back has been passed down through generations of supporters and recorded in print so they will never be forgotten.

That's how special it is to play for this club and that is why the players who wear the light blue jersey under my command must always realize the responsibility they have. They are idolized by those marvellous supporters in the magnificent Ibrox stands, who follow us around the country and beyond, wherever we may play. A special kind of professional is needed by this club to justify that kind of backing and that is what I hope to create and build, with the assistance of so many people, at Ibrox.

This book chronicles 117 fantastic years for Rangers. I hope when another 100 years or so have passed, we will have achieved plenty more worth looking back upon with the same kind of pride. I wish this book every success, but I'm sure it needs no encouragement from me or anyone else. The very essence of what it contains will make it as much of a pleasure to the Rangers supporters all over the world as it is for me to write these opening words.

PRIZES GALORE   The awesome trophy room at Ibrox. It attracts visitors from all over the world every year and you can make dozens of visits and still not see every piece of silverware, item of memorabilia and all the souvenirs that are on show.

Introduction

'The Story of the Rangers ... is told because it is worth telling.' So wrote John Allan in his foreword to the very first history of Rangers Football Club, published in 1923. Now sixty-six years later, it is even more worthwhile a project to try and put the achievements and history of one of the world's most famous football clubs on record. If anything, John Allan, an eminent writer of his time, coined a real gem of an understatement. Since their birth 117 years ago, Rangers have become not just an amazingly successful football club, but an institution in Scotland, an integral part of the country's tradition and fabric. Unparalleled success in the Scottish game is something the very first Rangers side, on Flesher's Haugh back in 1872, could never have anticipated. That, though, is exactly what has been achieved, and the club are now looking to reach new heights and discover new horizons under the leadership of David Murray and Graeme Souness.

So what makes Rangers Football Club hold the significance it does, not just in footballing terms but in our society as a whole? Is it the traditions and ideals upon which the club was founded? Is it the numerous great players who have graced the light blue jersey? Is is the legendary figures who have filled the manager's chair, from William Wilton to Graeme Souness? I would beg to suggest that it is none of the above that makes and has made Rangers the force and presence they are today. No, it is the people without whom Rangers, or any other great club, would be little or nothing ... the supporters.

As the current chairman has often stressed, like many before him, Rangers belong to their fans. Fans who have followed them all over the world; fans whose lives revolve around the fortunes of the team; fans who rightly believe they are an important part of Rangers Football Club. It is because of the loyal supporters that this book has been published.

The last official history of the club was published in 1973 and much has happened in the subsequent years. Rangers have acquired an even greater stature in the world game with their extraordinary financial investments. Ibrox Stadium is undoubtedly one of the finest football arenas on the globe. Everything about the club these days is of the highest quality, and hopefully this book will match those standards.

Fleshers Haugh - Glasgow Green
First Home, 1873-1875

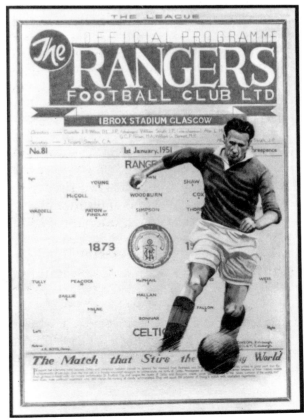

EARLY DAYS   The artist's impression of Flesher's Haugh, the site of Rangers first ground back in the days of their formation.

PROGRAMMED FOR SUCCESS   A stunning example of the work of Senga Murray, the artist commissioned by Rangers to portray the club's history with her unique drawings. This one shows Willie Waddell against the backdrop of a match programme from a pre-war 'Old Firm' fixture at Ibrox.

1
In the Beginning

Should Moses and Peter McNeil, William McBeath and Peter Campbell be looking down upon Ibrox Stadium from above, they are no doubt shaking their heads in awe and bewilderment.

Those four names will mean little to the youngsters who, in these exciting times for Rangers Football Club, walk with a spring in their step to the £12 million stadium where Graeme Souness leads his men to greater glories. But it was this quartet who, in their teenage innocence, built the foundations of one of the world's most extraordinary footballing institutions.

Little could they have imagined in the crisp spring of 1872, when they decided to leap upon the footballing bandwagon sweeping over Britain, that over a century later the club they gave birth to would be the most powerful and successful in the country. Yet it was these men and those they recruited upon Glasgow Green to join them who formed Rangers. Deriving the name from an English rugby union team he had heard of, Moses McNeil christened the new club with a name which is now known all over the world wherever football is played.

In those embryonic stages, Ibrox Park and big crowds were a long way off. It's not recorded how many people watched Rangers draw with Callander FC in their very first match in the spring of 1872, but you can be sure that they would have been outnumbered today by the stewards at matchdays alone!

The first Rangers teams were mostly made up of very young players, most of them still in their teens. Queen's Park, Scotland's oldest club which was formed in 1867, and Vale of Leven were the country's footballing giants and they simply refused to play the precocious young upstarts from Flesher's Haugh in those early years. And while that may sound arrogant, it really is a bit like Drumchapel Amateurs throwing down a challenge to the Rangers of today. However, it's unlikely that the lads from Drumchapel would achieve the result which Rangers did when Vale of Leven eventually agreed to take them on in 1873.

This was the year that Moses McNeil and his team-mates really made the somewhat toffee-nosed football establishment which had already developed in

Scotland sit up and take notice. The match was drawn, and when Rangers achieved the same result against Clydesdale, one of the game's other leading lights of the time, the people began to take a real interest in the lads in light blue. The colours, incidentally, were chosen unanimously in those early meetings and, apart from a brief spell of wearing hooped jerseys, they have remained the same to this day – notwithstanding, of course, the rather more sophisticated designs of recent years!

The Scottish Football Association had been formed in March 1873 and after these heartening results against the country's top sides, Rangers, although still without a ground to call their own, became members. So it was that in the 1874–75 season, Rangers made their début in competitive football with their first entry into the Scottish Cup.

The competition had started the previous season with Queen's Park, to no one's surprise, lifting the trophy. Rangers knew that if they could make an impression in the tournament they would eventually meet the giants from Hampden and then the mighty Queens would have to take them on. Sadly for the determined young Rangers, they would have to wait.

Rangers did win their first round tie, against Oxford 2–0. Moses McNeil and David Gibb scored the historic goals and the match, ironically, was played at the Queen's Park Recreation Ground from where the 'Spiders' had moved to Hampden a year before. Dumbarton, a club which would be one of Rangers greatest rivals in many of those formative years, were the hurdle in the second round, and after a goalless draw at Glasgow Green the men from Boghead won the replay by the game's only goal.

It's worth recalling the eleven men who took part in Rangers first ever competitive match: James Yuill, Peter McNeil (Captain), Tom Vallance, William McBeath, William McNeil, Moses McNeil, David Gibb, Peter Campbell, James Campbell, George Phillips, James Watson.

Rangers had now established themselves on the football scene but still they lacked the identity that owning a ground brings. In 1875, the problem appeared to be solved. The club left Flesher's Haugh upon Glasgow Green behind them and moved to the Burnbank ground just off Great Western Road. It didn't work out, with Rangers spending just the one year there – but that 1875–76 season at least saw the Light Blues at long last take on Queen's Park.

Rangers had again been disappointed in the Scottish Cup. After easily defeating First Lanark 7–0 at Burnbank in the first round, they made their exit once more in the next stage of the competition, losing 2–0 to an impressive Third Lanark side at Cathkin Park. All of that was forgotten, though, when the excited and confident Rangers players took the field at Hampden Park for their challenge match against the still unbeaten Queen's Park. They were given no chance and indeed lost the match 2–0. But such was the passion-filled performance of the young Rangers that afternoon, they emerged with massive credit and the roars of approval from the spectators ringing in their ears. Ever since then, Rangers have always been one of the best-supported, if not always *the* best-supported, teams in the country.

The Clydesdale Football and Cricket Club had vacated Kinning Park to take

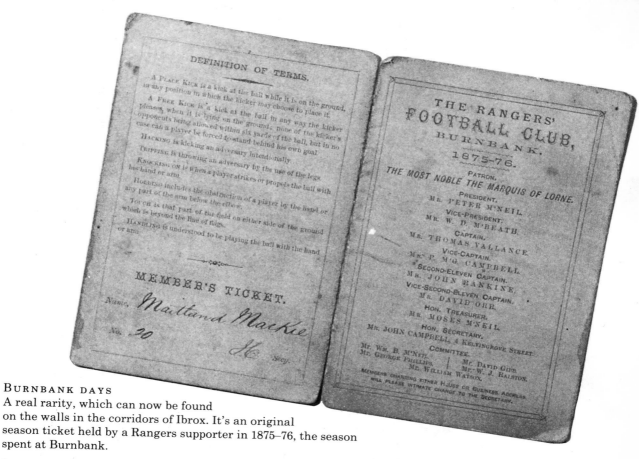

DEFINITION OF TERMS.

A PLACE KICK is a kick at the ball while it is on the ground, in any position in which the kicker may choose to place it.

A FREE KICK is a kick at the ball in any way the kicker pleases, when it is lying on the ground; none of the kicker's opponents being allowed within six yards of the ball, but in no case can a player be forced to stand behind his own goal.

HACKING is kicking an adversary intentionally.

TRIPPING is throwing an adversary by the use of the legs.

KNOCKING ON is when a player strikes or propels the ball with his hand or arm.

HOLDING includes the obstruction of a player by the hand or any part of the arm below the elbow.

TOUCH is that part of the field on either side of the ground which is beyond the line of flags.

HANDLING is understood to be playing the ball with the hand or arm.

MEMBER'S TICKET.

Name. *Maitland MacKie*

No. 20   Secy.

THE RANGERS'
FOOTBALL CLUB,
BURNBANK.
1875-76.

PATRON.
THE MOST NOBLE THE MARQUIS OF LORNE.

PRESIDENT.
MR. PETER M'NEIL.

VICE-PRESIDENT.
MR. W. D. M'BEATH.

CAPTAIN.
MR. THOMAS VALLANCE.

VICE-CAPTAIN.
MR. P. M'G. CAMPBELL.

SECOND-ELEVEN CAPTAIN.
MR. JOHN RANKINE.

VICE-SECOND-ELEVEN CAPTAIN.
MR. DAVID ORR.

HON. TREASURER.
MR. MOSES M'NEIL.

HON. SECRETARY.
MR. JOHN CAMPBELL, 4 KELVINGROVE STREET.

COMMITTEE.
MR. WM. B. M'NEIL.   MR. DAVID ORR.
MR. GEORGE PHILLIPS.   MR. W. J. RALSTON.
                    MR. WILLIAM WATSON.

MEMBERS CHANGING EITHER HOUSE OR BUSINESS ADDRESS WILL PLEASE INTIMATE CHANGE TO THE SECRETARY.

BURNBANK DAYS
A real rarity, which can now be found
on the walls in the corridors of Ibrox. It's an original
season ticket held by a Rangers supporter in 1875–76, the season
spent at Burnbank.

SCOTTISH CUP PIONEERS   The Rangers side that played in the club's first Scottish Cup
final in 1876–77. *Back row*: George Gillespie, William McNeil, Tom Vallance, J. M. Watt. *Middle
row*: William Dunlop, David Hill, Peter Campbell, Moses McNeil, Sam Ricketts. *Front row*:
James A. K. Watson and A. Marshall.

up residence at Titwood Park, a ground they still use to this day, although now only as a cricket club. Kinning Park, just a long goal-kick away from the current Ibrox Stadium, seemed the ideal location for Rangers when they were forced to leave Burnbank.

That first season at Kinning Park, 1876–77, was a momentous one for the young Light Blues with their ever-growing reputation, as they reached the Scottish Cup final for the first time. They cruised through, by an admittedly easy route, beating Queen's Park Juniors (4–1), Towerhill (8–0), Mauchline (3–0) and Lennox (3–0). Their opponents in the final, held at Hamilton Crescent, the West of Scotland Cricket Club's ground, were Vale of Leven.

Vale were challenging Queen's Park for the title of Scotland's number one club and indeed had become the first team from north of the border to beat the Hampden men, achieving the feat by a 2–1 scoreline in the quarter-finals of the Scottish Cup. So, quite clearly, they went into the match as red-hot favourites with the experts – yes, they had them even then (!) – predicting confidently that Vale of Leven's experience and physique would prove far too good for the youthful enthusiasm of Rangers.

Around 12,000 fans witnessed the match on 17 March and they saw Rangers stun the favourites with a spirited and stylish performance. Paton headed Vale of Leven into the lead midway through the second half and at that stage it looked enough to give them the cup in spite of Rangers' impressive display. But, showing a resilience and never-say-die attitude that would become the hallmark of the club in the seasons to come, Rangers equalized when Moses McNeil and Peter Campbell forced Vale centre-forward McDougall into putting the ball past his own keeper. The young pretenders left the field to a huge ovation and many of those who turned up for the replay, again at Hamilton Crescent, on 7 April were by now committed Rangers fans.

When William Dunlop fired Rangers into a seventh minute lead, it looked as though the new heroes of Scottish football were set to win the cup. However, Vale of Leven fought back tenaciously and in the opening minutes of the second half Baird equalized with the Rangers defence all over the place.

It was an absorbing contest, thoroughly enjoyed by the 14,000 crowd, but many of them were incensed by the incident in extra-time which would ultimately cost Rangers the trophy. William Dunlop appeared to have scored again when his shot of some ferocity clearly passed through the uprights before goalkeeper Wood booted it away. After consulting his touch umpires, referee James Kerr denied the nonplussed Rangers players what had seemed a legitimate winning goal.

Shortly after the match had ended, eminent Glasgow surgeon George McLeod confirmed Rangers' claims for a goal. He had been standing behind the goal and had seen the ball pass Wood, strike a spectator and rebound back into play before the Vale keeper made his clearance. It was an awful piece of misfortune for the young Rangers players who had given their all, but they summoned up their resources once again for the second replay at Hampden Park on Friday, 13 April.

Whether or not the players were superstitious or not isn't known, but it wasn't a lucky day for Rangers. McLintock opened the scoring direct from a corner-kick for Vale and they held on to their 1–0 advantage until half-time. Rangers, by now rid of the underdogs' tag, gave their growing army of fans in the 15,000 crowd great hope when they scored two quick goals in the second half through Peter Campbell and William McNeil. Sadly, the legs of the young Light Blues gave way as the ninety minutes drew to a close. Baird equalized for Vale and with a couple of minutes remaining, Paton grabbed the winner to give the favourites the Scottish Cup. The brave Rangers players slumped to their knees as the final whistle blew. But whatever their natural disappointment, they had made an indelible mark on Scottish football and from then on, the name of Rangers would command respect wherever they played.

Rangers were now making a name for themselves and the players were growing in experience and stature all the time. Only one thing was missing – that first elusive piece of silverware and when the Light Blues returned to Hampden Park on Saturday, 19 April 1879 for their second Scottish Cup final, controversy would dog them once more. Vale of Leven were the opponents once more, but Rangers were justifiably confident after having defeated Queen's Park 1–0 *en route* to the final.

Inspired by William Dunlop, Rangers started brilliantly and a fine solo goal from William Struthers gave them the lead. It then seemed Struthers had scored a second goal when he headed home a Dunlop cross just before half-time, but referee James Wallace from Beith angered the Rangers players when he disallowed the goal. He said Dunlop had been off-side when he crossed the ball, a decision that even puzzled the relieved Vale of Leven players.

Despite their fury, it seemed as though Rangers would hold on to their 1–0 advantage and lift the Scottish Cup – until a dramatic intervention by Vale two minutes from time. A corner-kick from Ferguson on the right fell to James McFarlane after an unholy scramble and his shot deceived Rangers' keeper, George Gillespie, who thought the ball was going wide, and it trickled inside the post for the equalizer.

Rangers felt badly aggrieved and in the days leading up to the scheduled replay a week later, the word got out that they were so furious, they were refusing to participate in the second match. True enough, Vale of Leven turned up to find no opponents at Hampden Park and they simply ran the ball up the park and knocked it into the empty net to win the Scottish Cup!

Rangers had protested officially to the Scottish Football Association without success, but a fortnight later they at least found some consolation. Rangers were to play Vale of Leven once again, this time in the final of the Glasgow Charity Cup. The Light Blues won the match 2–1, ironically the scoreline they claimed to have triumphed by in the Scottish Cup final. Skipper Tom Vallance took great pride in collecting Rangers' first ever trophy. It would be the only one they lifted in their first eighteen years – but it was the prelude to over a century of triumphs interspersed with controversy and anguish.

The seasons following that 1879 drama were anything but glorious for Rangers. Many of their best players were lured south of the border to the top English clubs who, despite their amateur billing, were paying great incentives.

Professionalism was not legalized in England until 1885 and in Scotland some eight years later, but there was no doubt that 'backhanders' south of Hadrian's Wall were commonplace.

Rangers tried hard to compete with their rich neighbours in England and in 1886–87 actually reached the semi-finals of the FA Cup, losing out to Aston Villa 3–1 at Crewe. Indeed, the summer of 1887 was a milestone for Rangers as they moved to the first version of their current home, Ibrox.

Kinning Park had become antiquated and was finally closed in February that year and when Rangers looked around for a new home, the district of Ibrox was seen as ideal. Situated next door to the current stadium, the first Ibrox was mainly the result of work by Fred Braby & Co of Petershill Road, Glasgow. The ground had an open stand with 1,200 seats and a one-storey pavilion, which resembled a small railway station.

A 15,000 crowd turned up for the official opening on 20 August 1887 and, although Rangers were happy with receipts of £290, an 8–1 defeat by English giants Preston North End did little to instil confidence in the players – especially as the match lasted just 45 minutes! Known as the 'Old Invincibles', Preston exposed Rangers on-field deficiencies to an alarming degree and it was clear there was much work to be done before the club could justify their large outlay on new premises.

The 1888–89 season summed up Rangers' plight. Of 39 matches played, they won just 13 and lost 19, conceding 108 goals in the process. Something special was needed and it arrived the following season in the shape of one William Wilton when he was appointed as match secretary.

Despite his title, Wilton was to all intents and purposes the first manager of Rangers Football Club and his presence would alter the course of the club on the honours trail in Scottish football. And he brought new players to Ibrox, notably Hugh McCreadie, David Mitchell and James Henderson.

If Wilton's arrival was significant for Rangers, so was the formation of the Scottish League in 1890. The eleven founder members started a competition that would strengthen Scottish football and lead to increased standards and competitiveness. Alongside Rangers in that first season, 1890–91, were Celtic, Third Lanark, Hearts, St Mirren, Dumbarton, Renton, Cowlairs, Cambuslang, Vale of Leven and Abercorn.

Rangers' first League fixture took place at Ibrox on 16 August 1890 when the following team defeated Hearts 5–2: Reid, Gow, Muir, Marshall, A. McCreadie, Mitchell, Wylie, Kerr, H. McCreadie, McPherson, Hislop. The first title race was an exciting one and when the fixtures had been completed, Rangers and Dumbarton tied at the top of the table with twenty-nine points each. A play-off was sanctioned, but despite leading 2–0 at one stage, Rangers could only draw 2–2 with the Boghead men at Cathkin Park on Thursday, 21 May and it was decided that the Championship would be shared.

It was around this time that Rangers great rivalry with Celtic took its roots. The East End club had been formed in 1887 and the first game between the teams had resulted in a 5–2 win for the Celts. Rangers, in fact, did not win an 'Old Firm' clash until beating Celtic 3–1 in the Glasgow Cup final of 1892–93 –

WILLIAM WILTON   To all
intents and purposes, the first
manager of Rangers Football Club.
A real gentleman of the Victorian
era, Wilton firmly put the club to
the forefront of Scottish football
and made the inspirational
appointment of Bill Struth as
trainer. When Wilton met a tragic
death by drowning at Inverkip in
1920, Struth took over the reigns
and and led Rangers to glories his
predecessor would have enjoyed
greatly.

A SILVER LINING   A famous
Rangers side line-up for the Victorian cameraman after beating
Celtic 3–1 to win the Scottish Cup
for the first time (1894). The Glasgow Cup is also in the picture and
the air of dominance beginning to
be assumed by Rangers can almost
be seen on the face of manager
William Wilton in the centre of the
photo. Trainer James Taylor is at
the back. *Back row*: H. McCreadie,
J. Steel, N. Smith, D. Haddow, D.
Mitchell. *Sitting*: A. McCreadie, D.
Boyd, W. Wilton, J. Drummond, J.
MacPherson, J. Barker. *Front row*:
R. Marshall and J. Gray.

JOCK DRUMMOND   Signed from Falkirk in March 1892, Drummond formed a legendary full-back partnership with Nick Smith and shared many domestic and international honours with him. He wore a cap while playing, the last outfield man to do so in Scotland, and was a fearsome figure for any opposing left-winger. Jock was capped fourteen times for Scotland and later went back to Falkirk in a coaching capacity.

NEIL GIBSON   A brilliant half-back, one of the finest and most arrogant the Scottish game has seen. Born in Larkhall, Neil joined Rangers in 1894 from Royal Albert and was an outstanding performer in a ten-year spell with the club, which brought him four League Championship and three Scottish Cup winner medals.

Above **ALEX SMITH**   A true Ibrox legend, the Ayrshire-born winger signed for Rangers in April 1894. He played for the club for just over twenty years on the left wing and many fans who witnessed him would argue long into the night that he would have been a match for his successor in the position, Alan Morton. Smith had pace, skill and was a supreme crosser of the ball. He made twenty appearances for Scotland and won every domestic honour in the game with Rangers. Alex died in November 1954.

also the first time the Light Blues had won that trophy.

Even more satisfying was Rangers first Scottish Cup triumph the following season when again Celtic were their opponents in the final. The Light Blues' side – built upon the rock of a full-back partnership of Nicol Smith and Jock Drummond, who would become legends in Ibrox folklore – was the best the club had yet produced. Inconsistency was their only weakness with a 5–0 victory over Celtic in the League being mixed with unexpected defeats against lesser clubs. The Parkhead men were the champions but in that Scottish Cup final of February 1894 they had no answer to an on-song Rangers side.

Hugh McCreadie, John Barker and James McPherson each scored in a thirteen-minute period in the second half to put the Ibrox men into a 3–0 lead and although Willie Maley pulled one back for Celtic, the cup was in Rangers' hands for the first time. It should have signalled a real glory period for Rangers, but surprisingly the fans had to endure two barren seasons on the trophy front. However, 1896–97 changed all that with the Scottish Cup, Glasgow Cup and Glasgow Charity Cup all landing at Ibrox.

Rangers had built a formidable side with Matthew Dickie proving their best keeper in a long time since signing from Renton, Neil Gibson establishing himself as the best half-back in Scotland and Alex Smith a favourite with the supporters with his dazzling wing play.

Success and Rangers were now becoming inextricably entwined, and after another Scottish Cup triumph in 1898, they then landed their first outright championship win – and how! The Light Blues created a record that stands to this day and will almost certainly never be repeated by any team. Rangers won all eighteen of their League fixtures to lift the title. Rangers actually lost in each of the three cup finals that season but nothing could take the shine from their extraordinary championship triumph.

The following season, Rangers not surprisingly retained their title and 1899–1900 was also significant for the move to the site of the current Ibrox Stadium.

The first Ibrox had become too small to cope with Rangers' ever growing number of supporters and the success of the club enabled them to create the new stadium, which was opened on 30 December 1899 with a 3–1 win over Hearts in an Inter City League match.

The dawn of the new century was bright for Rangers and they were champions for the third and fourth successive times in 1900–01 and 1901–02. But, sadly not for the first time, tragedy would befall Ibrox at the end of the latter season when the west terracing at the ground collapsed during a Scotland–England international. A total of twenty-five people were killed in the disaster that badly shook Rangers and forced them to reduce the capacity of the ground to 25,000 by 1905. That year also saw Rangers lose the championship to rivals Celtic in a play-off and the two major honours, the League and Scottish Cup, were becoming elusive once more for the Light Blues.

The 1908–09 season was a dramatic and significant one for the club. Just to show that current trends are far from new, goalkeeper Herbert Lock was signed from Southampton, becoming the first Englishman to be brought to Ibrox. The season also produced the ill-fated Scottish Cup final between the 'Old Firm'.

MYSTERY MEN   Little is known about this rare photograph from the Ibrox archives. It is definitely a shot of the first Ibrox site and it looks like a Scotland–England international match taking place.

Opposite above INVINCIBLE   The astonishing Rangers side that completed all eighteen of their Scottish league fixtures in 1898–99 without dropping a solitary point. They deserve their place in the hall of fame as one of the greatest teams ever to wear the light blue jerseys. *Back row*: Nick Smith (right-back), James Miller (half-back), James Miller (forward), David Crawford (left-back), J. Wilkie (forward), Matt Dickie (goalkeeper), James Taylor (trainer). *Front row*: James Campbell (forward), John MacPherson (forward), Andrew Sharp (forward), R. C. Hamilton (forward), Alex Smith (forward), Neil Gibson (half-back), Robert Neil (half-back), David Mitchell (half-back).

Above THE FAR PAVILION   A superb photograph from the Ibrox collection which shows the Ibrox pavilion in the background. The team in the foreground had won the Scottish Cup in 1902–03. Star men of the season included Finlay Speedie, an exciting forward, who was a favourite with the supporters. He was sold to Newcastle in 1906 for £600 – he is fourth from left in the front row.

Right DISASTER   A sketch from the *Daily Graphic* of 12 April 1902 depicting the Ibrox Disaster of that year. A total of twenty-five people were killed when part of the stand gave way during a Scotland–England international match.

It's the match now referred to as 'The Day They Burned Down Hampden'.

After a 2–2 draw, Rangers and Celtic tied once again in the replay, this time 1–1. Some of the players headed for the pavilion when the final whistle was blown, others lingered on the field unsure as to whether extra-time would be played. There had been speculation among the fans before the game that teams were deliberately drawing cup-ties in order to get the money from replays. As almost £4,000 had been taken from the final so far, this speculation seemed fact to many inside Hampden.

Whatever their reasoning, hundreds of fans spilled on to Hampden and made for the pavilion, demanding that extra-time should be played. Their path was blocked by around 100 policemen and there then started the biggest riot Scottish football has seen as young fans rushed to the Somerville Road end of the stadium and set alight the 27 pay-boxes there. The field was cut up, goal-posts smashed and souvenirs taken. Any intervention by the police was met by a barrage of sticks, stones and any other missiles the fans could get hold of. The riot lasted for two-and-a-half hours and 130 people, mainly policemen, were injured.

Rangers and Celtic were both horrified and proposed to the SFA that the final should be abandoned. Their request was happily agreed to and for the first and only time, the Scottish Cup and medals were withheld.

A month later, Rangers defeated Celtic 4–2 in the Charity Cup final at Parkhead, but the club were still not happy at their progress on the field. The championship had not been won since 1902 and the Scottish Cup had been absent from the Ibrox trophy room since 1903.

In the championship, at least, Rangers made amends in 1910–11 when they took the title for the sixth time. It was a fine performance, particularly in the 'Old Firm' fixtures, which were both played at Parkhead owing to ground alterations at Ibrox. The teams drew 1–1 in the first game and Celtic were then defeated 1–0 in what was officially their 'home' match. The inspiration for Rangers that season was centre-forward William Reid who scored 48 goals in 42 matches all told. Reid, in fact, was the most influential player as Rangers held on to the championship in the subsequent two seasons and he made ninety appearances in total in the three triumphant seasons.

The Scottish Cup, though, was beginning to be seen by their supporters as a jinx competition for Rangers and in those three League winning seasons, the club made early exits at the respective hands of Dundee, Clyde and Falkirk. Hibs were the tormentors in 1913–14 as the hoodoo continued with a third-round exit at Easter Road and the League Championship was lost to Celtic by a six-point margin.

The significance of football in people's lives, though, was put into proper perspective when the First World War cast its shadow over Europe in 1914. Rangers' hopes of glory, like those of football teams throughout the country, would be put to the back of the mind. But the story of the club was only just beginning to take shape and when light dawned once more in 1918, so too would a new era for Rangers....

2
The Wee Blue Devil and other Heroes

When the Great War ended, Rangers began a glorious chapter of success in their history. The springboard for this must be traced back to the end of the last pre-war season, 1913–14. It was then that the club mourned the death of James Wilson, who had been trainer at Ibrox for seventeen years and who was the invaluable right-hand man of manager William Wilton.

A professional runner in his youth, Wilson had been an expert at getting players to a peak of fitness, although his quietly-spoken nature ensured he never hit the headlines. In his time at the club as trainer, Rangers were Scottish champions seven times, Scottish Cup winners twice, Glasgow Cup winners on eight occasions and also lifted the Charity Cup six times. His contribution to the cause of Rangers was priceless and his untimely death presented William Wilton with the problem of finding a successor.

Wilton's choice would prove to be an inspirational one. Into the Ibrox fold as trainer came William Struth, a former top-class sprinter who had made his name in football at Clyde. He had taken the Shawfield club to the Scottish Cup final twice and Wilton was in no doubt that Struth could help him forge a new and successful quest for honours at Ibrox. However, the duo could not have imagined that the first four seasons they spent together would mean little, cast into insignificance by the battles raging in Europe. Indeed, Wilton and Struth pushed aside their commitments with Rangers to pursue voluntary work at Bellahouston Hospital, helping to care for the men who returned wounded from foreign fields.

Football continued, with teams naturally weakened as players made their way to the recruiting offices, and apart from lifting the championship and Glasgow Cup in 1917–18, Rangers failed to collect any of the somewhat hollow honours available.

However, the years of war did see several significant additions to the Ibrox playing-staff, men who would play a major role in the exciting times which lay ahead. Full-back Bob Manderson from Northern Ireland first wore light blue in 1915, as did inside-left Andy Cunningham who joined Rangers from Kilmarnock.

A brilliant inside forward, Cunningham possessed uncanny close control and would go on to be one of Rangers' greatest ever captains. Two years later, right-winger Sandy Archibald, inside-forward Tommy Muirhead and half-back Arthur Dixon all arrived at Ibrox and each would carve themselves a niche in the club's history.

From the club's point of view, the most memorable day of the war years was 18 September 1917 when King George V held an investiture on the field at Ibrox.

Mercifully, hostilities in Europe ended the following year and Scottish football was facing an exciting new era once the start of the 1919–20 season came round. Servicemen returning from war were eager for entertainment and attendances were up all over the country. Much was expected of the new-look Rangers by their huge army of fans.

The Light Blues of William Wilton and Bill Struth didn't disappoint and in 1919–20 they were crowned champions with only two defeats suffered in their forty-two matches. They rattled in 106 goals and conceded just 25 with Andy Cunningham finding the back of the net 31 times in the course of the season. There was disappointment in the Scottish Cup once more as, after defeating Celtic 1–0 in the quarter-finals, Rangers were barred from Hampden by Albion Rovers who eventually won a three-match marathon in the semi-final. However, Rangers were on a high with average crowds at Ibrox of 30,000 and an income for the season of £50,946 which broke all existing Scottish football records.

At the end of the season, everyone at Ibrox was struck dumb with grief when William Wilton died, victim of a freak drowning accident. The man who had pushed Rangers to the forefront of Scottish football had gone – how would the void he left be filled?

The club's directors didn't have to search far for a replacement and in June 1920 they appointed Bill Struth as the new manager of Rangers Football Club. Struth had already made his presence felt at Rangers and in bringing him to Ibrox, William Wilton had effectively appointed his own successor. The man would become legend and in his first season in charge, 1920–21, he gave the club's supporters a taste of what was to come.

Rangers swept to the title again, finishing ten points clear of Celtic in second place and losing just one of their forty-two matches. It was an extraordinary feat and the team were compared to the great side of 1898–99 who completed their eighteen match League programme with a 100 per cent record. The season was also significant for the introduction of the man who is arguably the greatest player ever to have worn the light blue jersey – Alan Morton.

Christened 'The Wee Blue Devil' by English sportswriters in subsequent years owing to his eleven devastating appearances for Scotland against the 'Auld Enemy', the flying left-winger was brought to Ibrox from Queen's Park. His dancing, weaving, darting skills immediately endeared him to the Rangers fans and few defences could cope with his dazzling wing play, the peer of which had never been seen before and has never been matched since.

Morton hardly had the look of greatness about him, standing just five feet four inches tall and weighing in at only nine stone. He possessed astonishing

Left FOR KING AND COUNTRY Ibrox was the venue in 1917 for a Royal Investiture and here a soldier receives a medal from the King in front of thousands of Glasgow citizens.

Below left ANDY CUNNINGHAM A brilliant inside-forward, Cunningham was equally adept at scoring goals as creating them. He was signed from Kilmarnock in 1915 and won seven League Championships and one Scottish Cup winners medals with Rangers.

Below ALAN MORTON 'The Wee Blue Devil'. Christened this by a perplexed English sportswriter after another memorable display at Wembley for Scotland, Morton was a pure footballing genius. He gave Rangers magnificent service after signing from Queen's Park in 1920 and once he retired in 1933, he was a director of the club until shortly before his death in 1971. He was capped thirty-one times for Scotland, an amazing tally at that time, and consistently uplifted Scottish spirits with match-winning displays against England.

Alan L. Morton

Above DAVID MEIKLEJOHN A legendary captain, many *aficionados* reckon 'Meek' to be the greatest Ranger of all time. Willie Thornton is one and says of his former captain: 'He was the greatest player I ever saw.' He was signed from Maryhill Juniors in 1919 and remained at Ibrox until retiring in 1937. Meiklejohn won an astonishing haul of eleven League Championship and five Scottish Cup winners medals and was capped fifteen times for Scotland.

Left TOM CAIRNS Signed from St Johnstone in 1913, Cairns spent fourteen years at Ibrox and formed a formidable left-wing partnership with the great Alan Morton. He won seven League Championship medals with Rangers and deserved far greater credit for his contribution to the cause. Capped eight times for Scotland, Cairns went to Bradford City in 1927 and played senior football until he was forty-one.

balance, though, and wore just three studs instead of the normal four on the sole of each boot to give himself extra mobility. Full-backs had nightmares about him. Naturally right-footed, that didn't make his twists and turns any the easier to predict and he once likened his uncanny ability to possessing a sideview mirror on a car. Whatever his secret, there is no doubting Alan Morton was a soccer genius and his imposing portrait still looks down upon all who pass through the marble doorway at Ibrox today.

In that first season, Alan Morton created goal after goal for strikers Andy Cunningham, George Henderson and Tom Cairns and also chipped in with nine himself. The forward line of Archibald, Cunningham, Henderson, Cairns and Morton wreaked havoc with defences all over the country. But even they could do little to help Rangers add any of the three cup competitions to the championship. They were defeated by Celtic in both the Glasgow Cup and Charity Cup, but it seemed as though Bill Struth had ended the Scottish Cup jinx.

Rangers made it to the final and were hot favourites to defeat Partick Thistle and win the trophy for the first time since 1903. A first half goal from John Blair, Thistle's right-winger, was the only strike of the game and Rangers would have to wait longer to smash the hoodoo. It was the competition the Rangers fans most of all wanted to see their heroes win, but the following season there was further disappointment as the final was again reached, only for a superb free-kick from Jamie Gourlay to beat keeper Willie Robb and give Morton the cup.

The Scottish Cup and Rangers just didn't get on. In 1922–23, Ayr United defeated the Light Blues 2–0 at Somerset Park in the second round to stretch the jinx to twenty years. Rangers more than made up for it, though, by celebrating their fiftieth Jubilee season with a twelfth championship win, success in the Glasgow Cup for the fifteenth time and lifting the Charity Cup for the eleventh time.

Establishing himself as a firm fixture in the first team at this time was David Meiklejohn, a marvellous defender who was signed as a nineteen-year-old from Maryhill Juniors in 1919. One of Rangers greatest ever captains, 'Meek' went on to make 635 appearances in the light blue and also captained Scotland in several of his fifteen caps for his country. He was a huge influence in the side that was entering a real glory period, interrupted only by the 1925–26 season when an horrific injury list saw Rangers finish sixth in the League table, their worst ever position since the competition began in 1890.

The season, though, was not without its positive points for the club as three players arrived who would be vital cogs in the Ibrox machinery. Full-back Dougie Gray was snapped up from the unlikely outpost of Aberdeen Mugiemoss; inside-right Jimmy Marshall, a doctor by profession, was signed from Shettleston; and centre-forward Jimmy Fleming, a prolific scorer, was captured from St Johnstone.

The following season, the championship was reclaimed with some style and would be the first of five consecutive title triumphs by the Light Blues. It was also the swansong for Tommy Cairns, Arthur Dixon and Bert Manderson, who

Above THE BIG STRETCH   Brilliant Celtic goalkeeper John Thomson denies Rangers strikers Bob McPhail, Jimmy Fleming and Jimmy Smith on this occasion.

Left WEE DEVILS   These young Rangers fans find a way of getting into the 1928 Scottish Cup final without paying – it was worth the effort.

Above THE HOODOO BUSTERS   The management and playing-staff of that famous 1927–28 season. *Back row*: Bailie Duncan Graham (director), Bailie James Buchanan (chairman), James Bowie (director), William Rogers Simpson (secretary). *Middle row*: Sandy Archibald, Jimmy Fleming, David Meiklejohn, Tom Hamilton, Andy Cunningham, Bob 'Newry' Hamilton, Jock Buchanan. *Front row*: Bill Struth (manager), Dougie Gray, Tully Craig, Tommy Muirhead, Bob McPhail, Alan Morton, James Kerr (trainer).

Right THE MOMENT THE JINX ENDED   John Thomson is beaten at Hampden in 1928, but the Celtic captain, Willie McStay, fists the ball off the line. David Meiklejohn stepped up to score with the penalty and the rest is Ibrox legend.

'GREATEST EVER RANGERS'
1929-1930

1929-30

Above HIDDEN HERO Bob McPhail, partly obscured by the woodwork, scores Rangers' second goal in the famous final.

Left THE CLEAN SWEEP This picture pays tribute to the side named 'Greatest Ever Rangers' when they won every honour in the Scottish game during season 1929–30.

Opposite above GRAND SLAM The Rangers squad who cleaned up the domestic honours in 1929–30, winning the League Championship, Scottish Cup, Glasgow Cup and Charity Cup. *Back row*: James Kerr (trainer), David Meiklejohn, Jimmy Fleming, Sandy Archibald, Jimmy Fleming, Tom Hamilton, Jock Buchanan, Tully Craig, Bill Struth (manager). *Front row*: George Brown, Dougie Gray, Bob McDonald, Tommy Muirhead, Bob McPhail, Bob Hamilton, Billy Nicholson, Alan Morton.

Opposite below DANISH BLUES An unusual photo of the Rangers squad, taken on a close season tour in Copenhagen in the early 1930s.

BILLY McCANDLESS A popular full-back, known as 'Bucksy' to the fans. McCandless was an international of some renown with Northern Ireland.

SANDY ARCHIBALD Recalled mostly for his two goals against Celtic in the 1928 final, right-winger Archibald contributed far more than that to the Ibrox cause. The Fifer was signed from Raith Rovers in 1917 for £250 and was an awesome sight when he sped down the wing, always finishing with an accurate cross or fierce shot. He was an idol of the terraces, not least because he always seemed to perform brilliantly in 'Old Firm' games – Celtic manager Willie Maley he was delighted when Archibald retired in 1934!

Opposite ALL ABOARD A dapper Rangers squad as they prepare to sail on a close season tour to Canada in 1930. *From the top, and left to right*: Tom Hamilton, Dougie Gray, Bob Hamilton, Jock Buchanan, David Meiklejohn, Tully Craig, Andy Cunningham, Jimmy Fleming, Bob McPhail, James Bowie, Sandy Archibald, James Kerr, Alan Morton, Bailie Duncan Graham and Bill Struth.

fittingly ended their Ibrox careers with another championship medal. As three 'greats' departed, enter on to the scene one of Scottish football's greatest goalscorers – Bob McPhail.

One of the game's true gentlemen, McPhail was signed from Airdrie on 18 April 1927 and went on to score 281 goals for Rangers from the inside-left position. Bob had won a Scottish Cup-winners' medal while with the Broomfield club in 1924 and he would play a major role in helping his new team-mates experience the same feeling.

Yes, 1927–28 was the season when the Scottish Cup jinx was at long last lifted and how the Rangers fans celebrated one of the greatest ninety minutes in the club's history.

The Ibrox men approached the final against Celtic at Hampden on 14 April 1928 in excellent form, needing just three points from their remaining three League fixtures to be champions once more. The Scottish Cup, though, was a different matter and although the Rangers fans in the record-breaking crowd of 118,115 were boisterous and cheerful, the twenty-five year absence of the famous trophy from their team's hands ensured they were not without trepidation.

Celtic were the cup holders and in the first half, it seemed the worst fears of the Rangers fans were being realized as the Parkhead men swept down on Tom Hamilton's goal. Only a brilliant display of goalkeeping from the Rangers number one kept the scoreline blank at half-time, and one astonishing point-blank save from a Connolly shot still ranks as one of the greatest made by a Rangers keeper. The rest of the players took inspiration from Hamilton and ten minutes into the second half, Rangers got their first positive break in twenty-five years of Scottish Cup football.

Alan Morton crossed from the left and Jimmy Fleming – scorer of 47 goals in 45 matches that season – fired the ball past Celtic keeper John Thomson, only for Parkhead skipper Willie McStay to fist the ball clear on the line. The Rangers players maintained that the ball had crossed the line before McStay's intervention, but referee Bell waved them away and awarded a penalty-kick.

It was one of Scottish football's most dramatic moments as Rangers captain David Meiklejohn took responsibility upon himself and stepped up to take the kick. In what seemed like an age, Meiklejohn placed the ball on the spot before calmly driving the ball out of Thomson's reach into the net. Rangers never looked back. Bob McPhail made it 2–0 and two goals from Sandy Archibald sealed a 4–0 triumph, which ranks amongst the greatest of all Rangers' performances.

It was a marvellous springboard for the Light Blues who clinched the title the following Monday with a 5–1 win over Kilmarnock at Ibrox, while Celtic were dropping a point against Partick Thistle at Firhill.

That summer, the victorious Rangers went on a ten-match tour of Canada and the United States where they thrilled the New World soccer fans, winning seven and drawing three of their games. They returned to clinch the title again in 1928–29, but the Scottish Cup was prised from their grasp once more when Kilmarnock defeated the Light Blues 2–0 in the final.

Above TOMMY MUIRHEAD Signed for the princely sum of £20 from Hibernian in 1917. Muirhead was a fine half-back who could also play in attack and he proved a great captain for Rangers. He scored 49 goals in 352 appearances for the club and collected eight League Championship medals. He sadly missed the 1928 Scottish cup final through injury but was awarded a medal.

Above right WILLIE WADDELL A brilliant right-winger, Waddell made a scoring and winning début against Arsenal as a sixteen-year-old. He served Rangers as a player for eighteen years, winning four League Championship, two Scottish Cup and two League Cup winners medals. His 558 matches reaped 143 goals and he supplied many more for team-mates, particularly the head of Willie Thornton. He retired in 1956, but would return to Ibrox in a different capacity....

Right ALEX VENTERS Signed from Cowdenbeath, Alex was one of the big stars in the Rangers line-up in the 1930s with his surging, fearless forward play.

ALEX VENTERS

However, there would be no quarter-of-a-century wait to collect the trophy this time around and it was reclaimed the following season.

It wasn't alone at Ibrox in 1929–30 – Rangers won every single trophy open to them! Known as the 'Clean Sweep', the championship, Glasgow Cup, Charity Cup, Second Eleven Cup and Alliance Championship were all added to the Scottish Cup.

The season also saw George Brown make his début for Rangers, an amazing player who was ahead of his time. Signed from Ashfield Juniors, Brown would walk into any modern-day team as a *libero*. He never booted the ball as was the way of so many half-backs of the time, preferring to stroke precise passes all over the field.

Another tour of North America was embarked upon and saw Rangers win all fourteen matches they played. A young and powerful striker called Jimmy Smith scored eighteen goals on the trip and made his first impression in the light blue jersey. He would go on to share in many more glories with the club, but that tour marked the end of the Ibrox line for left-back Billy McCandless and left-half Tommy Muirhead. Both have undeniable places in the club's Hall of Fame.

Bill Struth led Rangers happily and confidently into the 1930s, his shrewd management ensuring a steady flow of the best talent to Ibrox while he phased out some of the greats in dignified style.

A superb Motherwell side became Rangers' chief rivals in the early part of the decade and they broke the sequence of title wins by taking the championship to Fir Park in 1931–32.

Alan Morton played his final part on the field in the Rangers story the following season and although he made just seven appearances, it was fitting that the club should again win the championship. Appointed as a director of the club where he gave great service too, Morton hardly had a bad ninety minutes among the 495 games he played for Rangers and his contribution of 115 goals was superb for a winger.

Jock Buchanan, a stalwart at right-half since signing from Morton in 1927–28, also bowed out, but the mastery of Bill Struth's management was such that the departures of such key players went almost unnoticed as the success continued.

The 1933–34 season was a prime example. Jimmy Simpson, signed from Dundee United, established himself in the heart of the defence, while Billy Nicholson took up the unenviable task of following in Alan Morton's footsteps on the left wing with great aplomb. Rangers won everything in sight. The Scottish Cup was landed again and the 5–0 victory over St Mirren in the final was a personal triumph for Nicholson who scored twice and generally tormented the poor Saints defence. There was no team to match Rangers at this time and they were even unofficially crowned British champions when they defeated Herbert Chapman's great Arsenal side 2–0 at Ibrox and then drew 1–1 at Highbury.

A star in the team at the time was goalkeeper Jerry Dawson, who had taken over between the posts from Tom Hamilton. Signed from Camelon Juniors,

Dawson soon made his mark at international level with Scotland and became known as 'Prince of Goalkeepers'.

Rangers won the championship and Scottish Cup again in 1934–35 with the irrepressible Jimmy Smith scoring thirty-six goals in the League alone. Smith was a frightening sight for defenders, a huge tank of a man who, in the days when goalkeepers did not receive such blanket protection as they do now, chalked up many goals by forcing the keeper and the ball into the net at the same time!

Sandy Archibald, the winger who had provided Smith with many of his goals, brought down the curtain on his career at Ibrox in 1935 when he was sold back to Raith Rovers. Archibald was a magnificent servant for the Light Blues and particularly endeared himself to the Rangers supporters because of his consistent ability to play well in 'Old Firm' matches. Celtic manager of the time, Willie Maley, said that so long as Archibald was on the pitch, his side were never sure of beating Rangers no matter what the scoreline was. The first season without Celtic's chief tormentor, 1935–36, saw the Parkhead men win the championship for the first time since 1926.

Still Rangers managed to mark the season down as an historic one as they became the first team since the pre-professional days of Queen's Park to win the Scottish Cup three times in a row. The victories over St Mirren (1934) and Hamilton Accies (1935) were followed up successfully when Bob McPhail scored after just ninety seconds of the final against Third Lanark. It was the only goal of the match and it was fitting that McPhail should score the goal as it brought him a record seventh Scottish Cup-winners' medal.

It was also an emotional day for David Meiklejohn as he collected his last major honour with Rangers. He bowed out at the end of the season after 635 first-team appearances to leave the captaincy in the safe hands of Jimmy Simpson.

Simpson had the misfortune to lead Rangers when they suffered one of the biggest shocks in their history, being knocked out of the Scottish Cup in the first round in 1936–37 by Queen of the South at Palmerston Park. John Renwick was the player who scored the goal to make an unexpected name for himself, but while Celtic took advantage to go on and win the cup, Rangers recovered and lifted the championship for the twenty-third time.

One of the mainstays of the side by this time was inside-right Alec Venters. A player of great promise, Bill Struth had signed him from Cowdenbeath in November 1933 but a lack of self-confidence had held the player back. The Ibrox boss eventually instilled in Venters the vital belief in his own ability that was required and he went on to have a glorious career at the club, scoring 188 goals in 396 games, collecting four League Championship medals and being capped for Scotland.

A sixteen-year-old by the name of Willie Thornton made his first tentative steps on the first-team scene on 2 January 1937 as Bill Struth constructed a team destined for even greater heights. Despite his youth, the lad from Winchburgh quickly made his mark and although 1937–38 was a barren season for Rangers apart from their success in the Glasgow Cup, Thornton's progress excited all

GEORGE YOUNG   Signed from Kirkintilloch Rob Roy in 1941, 'Corky' was a Scottish foot-balling legend and his haul of fifty-three caps was a record for the Scotland team for many years. He captained the Scots on forty-eight of those occasions and his physical presence was quite awesome on and off the field. He captained Rangers to many great triumphs and possessed a lot of skill along with his powerful tackling ability. He retired in 1957 and later became manager of Third Lanark.

who watched him and he scored seven goals in twenty outings in his first full season.

Dougie Gray, Bob McPhail, Jimmy Simpson, Jimmy Smith, George Brown and Bob McDonald were all reaching the twilight of their careers and the injection of young blood like Thornton's was seen as a priority by Struth. With that in mind, Jock Shaw, Willie Waddell, Scot Symon, Jimmy Duncanson and Willie Woodburn were all brought into the Ibrox fold. They were all able to make their mark and learn the Rangers way while success was maintained with the championship being brought back to Ibrox in 1938–39.

Waddell was possibly the biggest star of the quintet and he had been earmarked for glory by Struth ever since he was a prococious fifteen-year-old and, indeed, he had played for Rangers reserves at that age. His first-team début at the start of the 1938–39 season was sensational – he scored the only goal of the game against English kings Arsenal in a friendly at Ibrox and gave England full-back Ernie Hapgood his most uncomfortable ninety minutes in a long time.

The fresh blood had been perfectly transfused by Bill Struth and there seemed no reason to doubt that his Rangers side were going to continue on their majestic way. Sadly, there was one eventuality that no one could plan for as the clubs prepared for the 1939–40 season. Britain declared war on Hitler's Germany on 3 September 1939 and once again the whole structure of football had to be changed as it became of secondary significance to even the most dedicated lover of the game.

BOBBY BROWN   The last line of the 'Iron Curtain' defence, Brown was an exceptional goalkeeper who had a lot of style. The strength of Rangers' back line at the time meant he wasn't always busy, but when called upon he made some astonishing saves. Bobby was signed from Queen's Park in 1946 and spent ten years at Ibrox before losing his place in the team to George Niven and joining Falkirk for £1,000.

SAMMY COX   An intelligent and technically superb left-back, Cox was a mainstay of the Rangers defence after signing from Dundee in 1946. He won twenty-four caps for Scotland and was one of the few full-backs in the world who consistently got the better of legendary English winger Stanley Matthews. Cox collected every domestic honour in the game with Rangers before leaving in 1956 to join East Fife.

TORRY GILLICK   A real crowd pleaser, Gillick was a dazzling inside-forward who could also play on the flanks. He had two spells with Rangers, first signing in 1933 from Petershill. Two years later he went to Everton for £8,000, but returned to Ibrox in 1945 where he spent another six years.

3
End of an Era

The Second World War was a harsh intrusion into the lives of everyone in the country and football suffered along with everything else. Rangers had been preparing for a golden era, in terms of triumphs and attendances. On 2 January 1939 Ibrox had held its greatest ever crowd, 118,567 spectators witnessing the 'Old Firm' clash, and the stadium was second in size only to Hampden Park in Britain.

In the seven seasons that the hostilities affected, Rangers won whatever championship was on offer. First of all the Regional League in 1939–40, followed by the Southern League Championship in the six seasons up until the last term of the war, 1945–46.

Football continued to provide entertainment for the beleaguered people and although there was never much semblance of a settled side, with so many on duty with the services, Rangers more than did their bit to satisfy the demand for relief from the day-to-day pressures of living in war-time.

The war years saw the end of the Ibrox career of George Brown, a massive on-field influence on the side since his introduction back in 1929. The cultured, thoughtful star hung up his boots in 1941 and promptly made a popular move from dressing-room to boardroom to become a director of the club. Brown made many significant contributions to the Rangers cause in his 417 first-team appearances and he would also prove a valued addition to the hierarchy at Ibrox.

Jimmy Duncanson was perhaps unfortunate to make his mark with Rangers during the war years when his talents in the inside-left position failed to attract the praise they deserved. The forward had a happy knack of scoring vital goals, and his stay at Ibrox at least extended four seasons beyond the end of the war and his 142 goals in 299 matches speaks for itself.

The 1941–42 season signalled the arrival of George Young and the defence that would become renowned as the 'Iron Curtain' began to take shape.

Signed from Kirkintilloch Rob Roy, Young was a giant of a man at six feet two inches and fifteen stone, but his size belied a skilful touch that allowed

Dynamic days A dramatic moment from the famous friendly match between Rangers and Moscow Dynamo in front of 90,000 fans at Ibrox in 1945 which ended in a 2–2 draw. Legendary Russian goalkeeper 'Tiger' Khomich is down injured with Rangers players Torry Gillick, Charlie Johnstone, Billy Williamson and Jimmy Duncanson looking on.

Jimmy Smith Signed from East Stirling in 1928, Smith was a prolific goalscorer for Rangers, netting 373 in League and Cup games before he retired in 1956. He had a reputation as a battering-ram centre-forward, but although he could certainly use his immense physical power to great effect, he also had a deft touch on the ball for a big man. He later served Rangers as a member of the coaching staff.

NET MINDER SUPREME Jock Shaw ushers a ball past the post with Jerry Dawson, arguably the greatest Rangers goalkeeper of all time, looking calmly on. Willie Thornton describes Dawson as 'the greatest keeper ever with astonishing reflexes and supreme confidence.' Dawson had exceptionally keen eyesight and his only weakness was his kicking. He signed from Camelon Juniors in 1929 and left to join Falkirk in 1945.

SCOT SYMON The player. Unlike his image as the dignified and quiet manager of later years at Ibrox, Scot was an aggressive wing-half during his playing career with the club. He signed from Portsmouth in 1938 and won a League Championship medal the following year only for his career to be interrupted by the war. He was a great passer of the ball, being able to win a tackle and find a team-mate with supreme style. He left in 1947 to manage East Fife.

him to add a new dimension to defensive play as centre-half and then right-back. His progress was severely jolted in 1943 when, opposed to Tommy Lawton in a Scotland–England international in Manchester, the famous English striker scored four goals in a crushing 8–0 defeat for the Scots. It was a stunning blow for Young, just twenty years old at the time, but his strength of character was displayed to the full by his subsequent recovery. He went on to prove himself one of Scotland's greatest ever internationals and his 53 caps are still a record for a Rangers player. Young captained Scotland in 48 of those appearances and that also remains as a record.

When the Victory Cup was competed for at the end of the 1945–46 season, that 'Iron Curtain' defence was nearing completion with the introduction of goalkeeper Bobby Brown and full-back Sam Cox. Rangers lifted that trophy with a 3–1 win over Hibs in the final and that was wholly appropriate, for the Easter Road men would be their greatest rivals in those early post-war years. Jimmy Duncanson scored two of the goals with Torry Gillick grabbing the other.

That season also saw one of the most revered matches in the history of Rangers take place, when the mighty Russian side Moscow Dynamo were the visitors to Ibrox on 28 November 1945. The Soviets were completing a four-match tour of Britain, which had already seen them defeat Arsenal and Cardiff City while drawing with Chelsea.

An all-ticket crowd of 90,000 packed inside Ibrox to see the glamour match and were stunned to see Karsev give Moscow Dynamo a 2–0 lead inside the first twenty-four minutes while a Willie Waddell penalty-kick was saved by Khomich. Rangers fought back wonderfully well, displaying a defiance in adversity and spirited commitment that would become a hallmark of the great side being created by Bill Struth. Jimmy Smith pulled a goal back and George Young notched the equalizer from the spot. Rangers even overcame a period when the Russians had twelve players on the field, having put on a substitute but failing to take another player off!

The line-up in the match was: Jerry Dawson, David Gray, Jock Shaw, Charlie Watkins, George Young, Scot Symon, Willie Waddell, Torry Gillick, Jimmy Smith, Billy Williamson, Charlie Johnstone. It was the end of an era for many of those players and jerseys number one to six were soon filled like this: Bobby Brown, George Young, Jock Shaw, Ian McColl, Willie Woodburn and Sam Cox. This was the original 'Iron Curtain' and how well it served the Light Blues.

The signing of Ian McColl from Queen's Park was the final brick in the wall that so many forward lines would find impregnable as Rangers went on to dominate Scottish football in the late 1940s and early 1950s.

The first season after the war, 1946–47, saw Rangers say goodbye to two magnificent servants, Dougie Gray and Jimmy Smith, and herald in a new period of excitement and glory. The championship was won by two points from the fine Hibernian side who gained revenge by knocking Rangers out of the Scottish Cup in the third round after a replay.

The big news of the season was the appearance of a third major domestic trophy for the clubs to play for, the Scottish League Cup. A gift from John

TREBLE KINGS The Rangers squad that became the first team to win the domestic treble of League Championship, Scottish Cup and League Cup. *Back row*: Bill Struth (manager), Willie Waddell, Ian McColl, George Young, Bobby Brown, Willie Woodburn, Willie Findlay, Willie Rae, Jimmy Duncanson, Jimmy Smith (trainer). *Front row*: Eddie Rutherford, Torry Gillick, Willie Thornton, Jock Shaw, Billy Williamson, Sammy Cox, Jimmy Caskie.

WILLIE THORNTON A goalscoring legend at Ibrox, Willie made his début for the club at the age of sixteen, having been spotted by Bill Struth as a prodigy with Winchburgh Albion. He was more than just a great header of a ball, which is the reputation handed down through the years. Thornton was as skilful a forward as any in the country and but for the war, he would have won more than the seven caps for Scotland he collected. Awarded the Military Medal for bravery during the war, he played with Rangers until 1954 and was Scotland's 'Player of the Year' in 1952. He later joined the Ibrox coaching staff after spells as manager of Dundee and Partick Thistle.

McMahon, then president of the Scottish League, Rangers romped to the final, defeating Hibs 3–1 on the way. The trophy was won in style, Aberdeen having no answer to Rangers in the Hampden final. Two goals from Jimmy Duncanson and others from Torry Gillick and Billy Williamson secured a 4–0 win.

At the end of the season, reliable left-half Scot Symon departed Ibrox to become manager of East Fife and he would have great success in the hot seat of the Bayview club. His absence from Govan was temporary – but more, much more, of that later.

In 1947–48, there was a role reversal as Hibs became champions by a two-point advantage over the Light Blues, but a Willie Thornton goal in the semi-final of the Scottish Cup against the Edinburgh men was enough to recompense Rangers. The 'Iron Curtain' really came into their own in this match – Hibs dominated for long periods but even their tremendous forward line could find no way through and one save by Bobby Brown from the great Gordon Smith was quite astonishing.

The ninety minutes at Hampden for the final was witnessed by an incredible crowd of 143,570 – a record to this day. Rangers duly won the Scottish Cup, but only after two dour, determinedly fought matches against a gritty Morton side. In the replay, it was a dramatic 115th minute goal from Billy Williamson, playing in his first Scottish Cup tie of the season, that finally sunk the Greenock men.

Willie Thornton was top scorer that season with twenty-six goals and the dynamic centre-forward, arguably the greatest header of a ball ever seen at Ibrox, bettered that by ten in 1948–49.

That season was a magnificent one from which Bill Struth must have taken great satisfaction as his well-oiled machine swept majestically to success in all three major honours. The championship was won on the last day with a 4–1 win over Albion Rovers. Willie Thornton scored a hat-trick and the title was clinched by a point from Dundee. Rangers eliminated Hibs from the League Cup in their qualifying section and went on to defeat Raith Rovers 2–0 in the final with Torry Gillick and Willie Paton grabbing the vital goals against the 'B' Division side. The first ever 'treble' in Scottish football was wrapped up. Clyde were the opposition at Hampden in the Scottish Cup final but could do little as Rangers, inspired by Willie Waddell, won 4–1 with goals from George Young (two penalties), Billy Williamson and Jimmy Duncanson.

Rangers completed a treble of a different kind the following season, 1949–50, when they repeated their Scottish Cup success to once again achieve the feat of winning the trophy in three consecutive seasons. Willie Findlay set the ball rolling after just thirty seconds with the opening goal of the final against East Fife, but the star of the show was Willie Thornton who led the front line magnificently. His two goals in two minutes in the second half sealed a 3–0 triumph and after the match, East Fife boss Scot Symon said of his old club: 'I've never seen Rangers play better.'

That cup final success was sweet revenge for Rangers as Symon's impressive East Fife side had ended their hold on the League Cup, winning 2–1 in the semi-final and going on to lift the trophy by beating Dunfermline in the final. Symon had clearly learnt his trade well under Struth at Ibrox as he also took the Methil club to a highly creditable fourth place in the championship that season. The title was won by the Light Blues for the twenty-seventh time, a 2–2 draw against Third Lanark at Cathkin Park clinching it by a solitary point from Hibs. By contrast, 1950–51 was a great disappointment as Rangers finished a massive ten points behind Hibs at the top of the League and were summarily dismissed at early stages of both cup competitions.

One shining light in a dim season was the arrival of Northern Ireland international striker Billy Simpson from Linfield in an £11,500 deal. Wisely played alongside the experienced Willie Thornton, Simpson learnt quickly and was an instant hit with the supporters, netting fourteen goals in his first season.

The likeable Ulsterman soon established himself in the side and forced out Billy Williamson, who was sold to St Mirren the following season. Simpson was unlucky with injury, though, and despite Willie Thornton maintaining his scoring rate with twenty-six goals, 1951–52 was another barren season for Rangers.

Bill Struth wasn't too despondent, not that he would accept anything but success from his Rangers sides, and the supporters did have some hugely enjoyable moments, none more so than the 4–1 victory over Celtic at Parkhead on New Year's Day. The Ibrox men were maintaining a supremacy over their 'Old Firm' rivals and it was disappointing that they should follow up a marvellous 3–0 win over the Celts in the League Cup semi-final by losing by the odd goal in five to Dundee in the final.

Rangers were fortunate at this time, as they have been throughout their history, to be blessed with a marvellously resilient and inspiring captain. The man in question here is Jock 'Tiger' Shaw and his nickname is best explained by the story of his part in that 4–1 Ne'erday win.

The second half of the match was underway with Shaw in the dressing-room, after being carried off with a bad leg injury following a clash with Charlie Tully. The left-back was almost completely immobile but pleaded with Bill Struth to let him join his team-mates back on the field. Struth refused, informing Shaw that the ten remaining were each putting in a little bit extra on his behalf, but there's no doubt the Ibrox supremo was proud of his skipper. Ironically, that injury would contribute to the end of Shaw's playing career at Ibrox and his place at left-back was eagerly taken by Johnny Little who had been signed from Queen's Park in July 1951.

Ian McColl and George Young were well able to follow on in the fine tradition of Rangers captains and the following season saw the glory trail rediscovered, the championship and Scottish Cup being landed.

Another signing from Queen's Park, Derek Grierson, was top scorer with thirty-one goals and Rangers also employed a new keeper. Bobby Brown was blamed for a disastrous 5–0 defeat by Hearts in the first match of the season – George Niven took over and never looked back. It was unfortunate for Brown but, just as in business, there is little room for sentiment in football. To Brown's credit, he battled with Niven all the way for his place until being sold to Falkirk in 1956 after 328 first-team appearances for Rangers.

When I said sentiment seldom has an important place in this game, it has to be stated that there were more than a few grown men shedding tears at Ibrox at the end of 1953–54. It wasn't because Rangers had been eliminated from both cup competitions at the semi-final stage or had finished fourth in the championship table, a distant nine points behind winners Celtic who collected their first title for 16 years. That was bad enough, but 1 April 1954 was no day for fooling around at Ibrox Stadium. After thirty-four glorious years as manager of Rangers, Bill Struth announced he was standing down from the position, although he would carry on as a director of the club. Well into his seventies, the great man felt the time was right to make way for a younger manager.

It truly was the end of an era for Rangers and a look at the stunning statistics of Struth's reign tells all that needs to be told: 18 League Championships; 10 Scottish Cups; 18 Glasgow Cups; 20 Charity Cups; 4 Southern League Cups; 2 League Cups; 7 War-Time Championships; 1 Victory Cup. Indubitably a remarkable honours list by any standards you may care to compare it with, and what a pity Struth did not have the chance to try his hand at guiding the club in European competition. A saying which has been repeated many times throughout the years is that 'no man is bigger than the club'. It's a maxim which has served Rangers well, but if any man came close to disproving its truth, it was Bill Struth. By the same token, he was always one of the first to insist upon its observance. It was a watershed of a season for Rangers and a month before Struth's dramatic announcement, on 3 March to be precise, John Lawrence was appointed to the board of directors. A new face in the boardroom is rarely a noteworthy landmark in the history of a club, but like his successor of current times, David Holmes, the arrival of Lawrence signalled a dramatic change in fortunes for Rangers.

John Lawrence's words on the day of his appointment summed up the man who had made his name as a huge success in the building trade: 'Rangers cannot, and never shall be, second best. No matter the cost, no matter the effort, and no matter the sacrifice, we shall go on to make Rangers respected and feared throughout the soccer world.' It was a clear indication of the drive of the man and along with Struth and the rest of the Ibrox board, they decided that Scot Symon would be the man to lead Rangers into a bright new era.

The former player, who had successfully made East Fife a respected name in Scottish football, was now in charge of Preston North End. He needed little persuasion to return to Ibrox, however, and on 15 June 1954 he became the third manager of Rangers Football Club.

The previous day, Rangers had returned from another successful tour of Canada and the United States and the club said goodbye to Jock Shaw and Willie Thornton. Shaw made 578 first-team appearances for the Light Blues and his never-say-die attitude was incredible throughout. Thornton rattled in 248 goals in 406 matches for the club and had his career not been interrupted by the war, in which he played a brave part, who knows what his tally would have been. He moved into the managerial chair at Dundee but would return to Ibrox in later years. The end of an era indeed – the Rangers fans awaited to see what chapter would now be written by the new men in control.

Top SILVER SMILES Jock Shaw is hoisted high by his team-mates after Rangers 1948 Scottish Cup final win over East Fife. *From left to right*: Bobby Brown, Willie Findlay, Willie Thornton, Ian McColl, Willie Woodburn, Jimmy Duncanson and Eddie Rutherford.

Left JOCK SHAW Another in a long line of great Rangers captains, 'Tiger' Shaw was a magnificent club servant.

Above DEREK GRIERSON Signed from Queen's Park in 1952, Derek was a goal-poacher supreme and was seen as the successor to Willie Thornton. He netted thirty-one goals in that first season, including this one against East Fife in a 4–0 win.

'POST WAR ERA' - The Light Blues Domination Continues............

Torry Gillick

Bobby Brown

Sammy Cox

IRON CURTAIN   The powerful Rangers side of the immediate post-Second World War period. Their defence was reputed to be almost impregnable and hence was named after the barriers being erected around Berlin at the time.

4

John Lawrence and
Scot Symon

Scot Symon's first season in charge of Rangers was notable for many things but sadly, a thirtieth Charity Cup success apart, the arrival of trophies at Ibrox was not among them.

Starting off with the League Cup campaign, the Light Blues won their qualifying section comfortably enough, although there was a heavy price to pay. Centre-half Willie Woodburn was sent off just thirty seconds from the end of the 2–0 win over Stirling Albion at Ibrox after clashing with Annfield forward Paterson. The robust defender from Edinburgh was never a favourite with referees, although many judges of the time felt his enthusiasm was too often mistaken for intentionally provocative play. Whatever the dubious merits of their decision, there was nothing Rangers or the devastated Woodburn could do when the Scottish Football Association imposed an indefinite ban on him.

There's no question that the twenty-four-times capped player was one of the Rangers greats, and in today's game his record of five dismissals in a long career would attract little adverse publicity. The weight of public opinion eventually saw the ban lifted two years later, but by that time Woodburn was thirty-six and any hopes of a comeback had vanished.

Scot Symon was fortunate that he simply had to move skipper George Young from his right-back role to the centre of the defence to fill the gap left by Woodburn's enforced departure.

Rangers finished the season as the only team in Britain to be undefeated at home in the League and their irresistible form at Ibrox included a 4–1 win over Celtic on New Year's Day. Billy Simpson opened the scoring and little South African winger Johnny Hubbard sank the Parkhead men with a hat-trick in the last eighteen minutes.

Rangers were far less impressive on their travels, and eight defeats ensured they finished just third in the League table, eight points behind champions Aberdeen. The Pittodrie men also ended the Light Blues' Scottish Cup aspirations with a 2–1 win in the sixth round.

Scot Symon knew he had to build for the future and that his Rangers side

WILLIE WOODBURN Signed from Musselburgh Athletic in 1937, Woodburn was a true colossus in the Scottish game and one of the finest centre-halves to play for Rangers and Scotland. Good in the air, good on the ground, Woodburn was capped twenty-four times for Scotland and won every domestic honour with the Light Blues. His *sine die* suspension in 1954 was a shattering blow for a man who fell foul of his own quick temper, but who was never known as a dirty player by fans or opponents.

BILLY SIMPSON Signed from Linfield for £11,500 in 1950, the Northern Ireland international striker was a prolific goalscorer who was popular with the Rangers supporters.

JIMMY MILLAR An inspirational striker, Jimmy was a bargain buy at just £5,000 from Dunfermline in 1955 and he was regularly Rangers' top scorer until leaving in 1967 for Dundee United. He possessed naturally good ball control and was quite tireless. His partnership with Ralph Brand was part of Ibrox legend.

ALEX SCOTT A brilliant right-winger, Alex was an idol of the Rangers supporters during his eight years at Ibrox. Signed from Bo'ness United in 1955, he had amazing pace and scored a lot of goals with his accurate and powerful shooting. Alex lost his place in the team to Willie Henderson and was sold to Everton for £39,000 in 1963 when he won English League and FA Cup winners medals to add to his complete collection of Scottish medals.

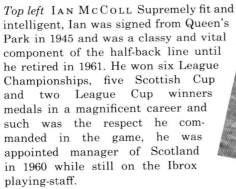

Top left IAN McCOLL Supremely fit and intelligent, Ian was signed from Queen's Park in 1945 and was a classy and vital component of the half-back line until he retired in 1961. He won six League Championships, five Scottish Cup and two League Cup winners medals in a magnificent career and such was the respect he commanded in the game, he was appointed manager of Scotland in 1960 while still on the Ibrox playing-staff.

Top right DON KICHENBRAND Signed from Delfos in 1955, Don was a powerhouse centre-forward from South Africa who thrilled the Rangers supporters with his up-and-at-'em style of play. Known as the 'Rhino', he scored twenty-nine goals in his first season but his time at Ibrox was short and he was transferred to Sunderland in 1958.

Above JOHNNY HUBBARD The South African winger arrived at Ibrox in 1949 and made an immediate impression on Bill Struth with his clever ball control and direct approach. He was a master from the penalty-spot, only missing twice in ten years with the club before he was sold to Bury for £6,000 in April 1959.

would have to be ready to face the new challenge being presented to Scottish clubs in the shape of European competition. Plans were announced for the introduction of the European Cup and the Fairs Cup in 1955, although it would be two seasons before Rangers would follow the initiative of Hibernian and step into the Continental arena.

Another of the old guard, striker Willie Findlay, joined Albion Rovers on a free transfer as Symon began the shake-up and two men for the future made their débuts in the second half of 1954–55. Centre-forward Jimmy Millar was signed from Dunfermline Athletic in January for £5,000 and while he would make a big impression in the years to come, it was eighteen-year-old Alex Scott who burst into the headlines immediately.

The right-winger, snapped up from Bo'ness United, made his début against his hometown club, Falkirk, at Ibrox on 9 March and devastated the Brockville men as he grabbed a hat-trick in Rangers' 4–1 win. A week later, the youngster catapulted himself into the national picture when he scored two goals in a 3–3 draw with Arsenal in a friendly at Highbury, prompting the London fans to draw comparisons with the legendary Alex James.

Scott was a major figure the following season, 1955–56, as Symon's restructuring process began to pay handsome dividends. Along with Ian McColl and Johnny Hubbard, the winger was an ever-present in Rangers' thirty-four-match League programme, which saw them recover from a poor start to win the championship for the twenty-ninth time.

A cult figure for the Ibrox fans was brought to the club in the shape of bustling centre-forward Don Kichenbrand. Known affectionately as 'The Rhino' for his less-than-subtle style of attacking, the South African was an instant success. He scored 23 goals in 25 League appearances and there's no doubt that the one cherished most by the supporters and Kichenbrand himself was the only strike of the New Year clash with Celtic at Parkhead.

Eric Caldow had started the season in the right-back role, but Scot Symon changed the formation at the rear by shrewdly signing Bobby Shearer from Hamilton Accies in December for £2,000. Shearer and Caldow, the latter switched to left-back, would go on to form a legendary partnership for Rangers, and the duo would also appear together four times for Scotland.

There was no joy in the cup competitions for the Light Blues, their League Cup and Scottish Cup ambitions ended by Aberdeen and Hearts respectively. But Symon could justifiably be satisfied with his first championship in charge of the club and entry into the 1956–57 European Cup.

Before that new ground was broken, it was farewell to two marvellous Rangers players. Willie Waddell and Sammy Cox were handed free transfers at the end of the season. Waddell had been at Ibrox since May 1938 while Cox had arrived in June 1946. Both were vital parts of the successful side of the late 1940s and early 1950s. The brilliant right-winger made over 550 appearances for Rangers and won seventeen official caps for Scotland. His international scroll of honour would have been far greater but for the war. Cox was a marvellously tenacious left-back, playing for his country twenty-five times and was greatly famed for his rare ability to keep the menace of Stanley Matthews at bay in Scotland–England clashes. The man from Darvel in Ayrshire played 349 times for Rangers and extended his career with East Fife before emigrating to Canada in 1959.

The date 24 October 1956 has huge significance in the history of Rangers. It was on that day that the club made their first appearance on the European stage. A crowd of 65,000 were inside Ibrox to see the Light Blues take on French champions Nice in the first round of the European Cup.

Faivre gave the Continental side the lead in the twenty-third minute but Rangers were by far the more powerful side on the night and they made their physical advantage count against the flair of their opponents. Max Murray and Billy Simpson scored the goals which gave the Ibrox men victory on their European début, but the margin of victory should have been far greater than that which they took with them to France.

Nice swapped finesse for fouls in the second leg on a sea of mud in France. It looked as though Johnny Hubbard had clinched the tie for Rangers with a fortieth-minute penalty-kick, but goals from Bravo and Foix evened the aggregate scores.

Luck completely ran out for Rangers in a play-off in Paris when they scorned chances galore before losing 3–1 to a Nice side who could count themselves fortunate over the three matches.

Still, the season had to be judged a success as Rangers put together a run of sixteen matches without defeat in the League to clinch their thirtieth championship by two points from Hearts, who had led for most of the contest. The fact that the Edinburgh club were beaten both home and away by the Ibrox men sealed the validity of their triumph. The vital fixture was in April at Tynecastle when Billy Simpson netted the only goal of the game. The Irishman shared a prolific fifty-goal partnership with Max Murray, which was crucial to the success.

Double success in the League was also enjoyed against Celtic, with 2–0 triumphs at both Parkhead and Ibrox, but it was the 'Old Firm' rivals who ended Rangers interest in both cup competitions.

The men from the East End were to cause Rangers and their supporters even greater heartache the following season – 1957–58 was not one to recall with any relish!

The Light Blues were devastated at Hampden in the League Cup final on an afternoon that would haunt them for years to come. Celtic won 7–1 – there is little that can be added to the scoreline which would give a clearer picture of the effects it had.

The championship was lost to an extraordinary Hearts side who finished a massive thirteen points clear of runners-up Rangers and scored 132 goals in their thirty-four matches.

The other half of the Edinburgh duo, Hibs, caused the frowns to be deepened on the brows of the Rangers players in the Scottish Cup. Yet to this day the players who lined up in that semi-final replay maintain that Max Murray's eighty-eighth-minute goal when Hibs led 2–1 was legitimate. It was a controversial moment of the highest profile and somehow typical of the fortune

MAX MURRAY   An unpredictable striker, Max was signed from Queen's Park in 1955 and although he scored plenty of goals in a Rangers jersey, he was never fully accepted by the fans. Brilliant one minute, he could miss the simplest of chances the next and when Jimmy Millar appeared on the scene, he was sold to West Bromwich Albion for £15,000 in 1962.

IAN McMILLAN   Known as 'The Wee Prime Minister', Ian was a cultured midfield player who complemented Jim Baxter superbly in that great Rangers side of the early 1960s. He was signed from Airdrie in 1958 for £10,000, winning every honour before going back to the Broomfield club for half the original fee in 1964.

experienced by Scot Symon's team during the season.

At least a first victory in the European Cup was recorded as French champions St Etienne were edged out 4–3 on aggregate. Sadly, the slick A C Milan were just far too good for Rangers in the second round and the 6–1 overall scoreline told its own stark story for the Ibrox management.

It was time for reappraisal and there were plenty of departures and arrivals as Rangers recognized the need to try to catch up on the ground lost to the top Continental sides. Andy Matthew, Bill Paterson and Ian McMillan arrived from East Fife, Newcastle United and Airdrie respectively and while the latter signing would be by far the most effective, the others would play their part in Scot Symon's shuffling of his pack. It was goodbye to Billy Simpson and Johnny Hubbard in 1958–59, as well, and both would be remembered with great affection by all Rangers fans.

Symon's methods were justified as the 1958–59 title was regained in dramatic style from Hearts. Rangers actually lost 2–1 at home to Aberdeen on the final day, but the Edinburgh club's defeat at Parkhead meant the two-point gap remained unaltered. The very thought of Celtic having contributed to a Rangers triumph made it all the more fun for the Rangers fans! Most important of all to Scot Symon, the championship success meant a swift return to European Cup action, but he was determined not to let the season pass without his players gaining more experience of facing foreign opposition.

Left-winger Davie Wilson, who had broken into the first team two seasons earlier after being signed from Baillieston, showed his love of the big stage with a magnificent display against Napoli under the Ibrox floodlights. Wilson scored twice in Rangers impressive 5–2 win over the Italians and Swiss side Grasshoppers were also beaten in Glasgow.

Those challenge matches were vital and a 3–0 win over Arsenal at Highbury, with new signing Ian McMillan orchestrating the play, was another sign that Symon was on the right track in his bid to make an impact in Europe with Rangers.

And make an impact they did the following season, although Rangers' ultimate departure from the European Cup at the semi-final stage emphasized the gulf they still had to cross.

Only the thuggish behaviour of their opponents worried Rangers when they took on Belgian champions Anderlecht in the preliminary round and the eventual 7–2 aggregate victory didn't flatter them.

Rangers were never far from drama in a European Cup campaign which caught the imagination of their supporters. Some 80,000 of them were inside Ibrox for the first leg of their first-round tie against Red Star Bratislava. It was a pulsating match in which Rangers scored goals in the first and last minutes, Jimmy Millar's last-gasp strike clinching a 4–3 victory. Czech defender Matalak was sent-off for striking Sammy Baird when it had actually been Tichy who delivered the blow and to cap it all Eric Caldow missed a penalty-kick.

It was Rangers' turn to have a player ordered off in the second leg, Jimmy Millar the culprit for retaliation. Happily, Alex Scott's goal earned a 1–1 draw and an overall win.

Holland was the destination in the quarter-finals and the astonishing script of the bid for glory continued apace. Rangers confounded the critics with a superb 3–2 win over Sparta Rotterdam in The Netherlands with goals from Davie Wilson, Sammy Baird and Max Murray. It left the Light Blues seemingly set up for a place in the semi-finals, but the second leg at Ibrox just a week later turned out to be a valuable European lesson.

Sparta showed Rangers that the home tie in Europe is not necessarily the easiest. Urged on by 82,587 fans, the Ibrox men put goalkeeper Van Dijk under extreme pressure but the killer touch was missing on a night of frustration. Van Ede stuck the only goal of the match past the exposed Billy Ritchie in the seventy-third minute as Sparta counter-attacked in devastating style. The days of the away-goals rule were still to come and the tied aggregate score meant a play-off and Highbury – a ground holding happy memories for Rangers – was named as the venue.

The Dutch champions had regained the initiative in winning at Ibrox and they further stunned Rangers by taking a seventh minute lead in North London through Verhoeven. The Sparta number four was not in such high spirits some nineteen minutes later when he sliced a Davie Wilson free-kick into his own net. It might have been a lucky equalizer but Rangers deserved to be level and the subtle and incisive promptings of Ian McMillan had turned the tide back in their favour. Sammy Baird gave Rangers the lead and when Van der Lee directed the second own goal of the night past a disgusted Van Dijk, the game was up for the Rotterdam side. Bosselaar pulled one back from the penalty-spot, but no one could deny that Rangers were worth their place in the last four on the strength of their displays over the three matches.

There was no doubt that Scot Symon's men found themselves in esteemed company in the semi-finals. European Cup holders and seemingly invincible Real Madrid from Spain; fellow Spaniards and Fairs Cup holders Barcelona; West German champions Eintracht Frankfurt – it was an achievement for Scot Symon's side to have been bracketed with them.

When the draw paired the Light Blues with the men from Frankfurt, it was viewed as the kindest possible outcome for them. How the Germans were underestimated!

Quite simply, Rangers were taught a footballing lesson of the highest order by Eintracht. The players were totally unprepared for the precise and dynamic brand of football which awaited them in Germany in the first leg and the 6–1 win for the home side was in no way flattering. Rangers were caught short in almost every department and were left with just pride to play for in the second match at Ibrox.

Still, 70,000 fans filled Ibrox, not just to support Rangers, but to enjoy the craft and mastery of the Teutonic team. Ian McMillan scored twice and Davie Wilson once for the Light Blues, but still their opponents were able to rattle in another half-dozen to leave Scot Symon pondering how much he still had to do to present a credible challenge in Europe. And even Eintracht didn't represent the pinnacle of European style. In an unforgettable final at Hampden, they were overcome 7–3 by magnificent Real Madrid in front of 135,000 fans.

Above BILLY RITCHIE Known as the 'Quiet Man' at Ibrox, Ritchie was just that off the field but an outstanding goalkeeper on it. Some of his performances were positively fantastic and it was a travesty that he won just one cap for Scotland. Signed from Bathgate Thistle in 1955, Billy won every honour in the game and left in 1968 to join Partick Thistle.

Left SAMMY BAIRD A rugged midfield player, Sammy's aggressive style and ability to score vital goals proved invaluable to Rangers in their early days in European competition. He was signed for £10,000 from Preston North End in 1955 and won all the domestic honours available with Rangers before joining Hibernian for £5,000 in 1960. He was capped seven times for Scotland.

Opposite BLONDE BOMBSHELL Davie Wilson has a shot saved by Celtic keeper Frank Haffey during the 1963 Scottish Cup final which Rangers won. He was signed from Baillieston in 1956 and spent eleven years at Ibrox, thrilling the fans with his lightning bursts of speed down the left wing – he also scored plenty of goals, including six in one match against Falkirk. He left Ibrox in 1967 and continued to play well for Dundee United and then Dumbarton.

Rangers gutsy but ultimately flawed European campaign cost them dear in terms of the championship and that 1959–60 title was won by Hearts, who finished twelve points ahead of the third-placed Ibrox men. The League Cup was a wash-out too, but the season had ample compensation in the shape of an exciting and successful Scottish Cup run.

Berwick Rangers, Arbroath and Stenhousemuir were easily bypassed before Jimmy Millar, top scorer in the term with thirty-eight goals, grabbed the winner against Hibs at Ibrox in a five-goal quarter-final.

Millar, in fact, had an extraordinary season and Celtic especially must have hated the sight of the man. When the Scottish Cup semi-final draw paired the 'Old Firm' together, Rangers had already beaten Celtic home and away with Jimmy Millar on target on each occasion in the League. The centre-forward thrived on the service provided by Alex Scott, Ian McMillan and Davie Wilson and he consistently gave the Parkhead defenders nightmares.

Celtic sensed that their luck had to change and when Steve Chalmers gave them a twenty-fifth minute lead at Hampden on 2 April, they must have thought that the Scottish Cup final beckoned. But Rangers were in no mood to let such a dramatic season slip by without landing a major trophy and in a second-half onslaught, Jimmy Millar scored an extraordinary equalizer, heading past Frank Haffey from all of sixteen yards out.

It was Haffey who kept Celtic's hopes alive with several superb saves but in the replay four days later, even he could not stop rampant Rangers. Davie Wilson scored twice as did – yes, you've guessed it – Jimmy Millar and the 4–1 win was a fair reflection for Scot Symon's men.

Kilmarnock, emerging as a potent force under the management of former Rangers' hero Willie Waddell, were the opponents in the final. In the end, the crowd of 108,017 seemed to intimidate the Ayrshire side at Hampden and as soon as Jimmy Millar had headed Rangers into a twenty-second minute lead, there was little doubt about the outcome. It was only fitting that Millar should score again in the sixty-eighth minute to complete the 2–0 win and he received an especially warm salute from the jubilant Rangers fans.

The triumph, Rangers fifteenth in the Scottish Cup, was just reward for the players after a real slog of a season and new vice-chairman John Lawrence praised them for 'making the critics eat their words'. But as he basked in the success of Hampden, Lawrence knew as well as Scot Symon that the rebuilding programme was only just beginning. Rangers had to make their mark much further afield. The dawn of the 1960s would bring new dramas and take the club much closer to their ambitions.

5
The Swinging Sixties

Any argument or discussion on the subject of the greatest player ever to play for Rangers will ultimately reach a stalemate. So many different supporters of different generations will advocate a particular favourite. Alan Morton, George Young, John Greig and Davie Cooper would all have their cases put forward by the many who have idolized them. In time to come, no doubt the likes of Ally McCoist, Terry Butcher and Ian Durrant will be regarded as the 'greatest' by a large number of today's fans. That's why in an earlier part of this book, Alan Morton was described as 'arguably' the greatest of them all.

Perhaps Morton's most obvious challenger for that title appeared on the scene on 21 June 1960. That was the day that Jim Baxter arrived at Ibrox Park to complete his transfer to Rangers from Raith Rovers for a then Scottish record fee of £17,500. It was money well spent as Scot Symon picked up the biggest bargain buy any club could hope for. Baxter was a footballing phenomenon and although he would be at Ibrox for just five seasons before moving to English football, it was a period relished by every Rangers fan who witnessed it.

'Slim Jim' was just twenty-one when he arrived in Glasgow and quite literally had the world at his feet. Perhaps that should read in the singular, for such was the world-class skill contained in Baxter's left foot, he only used his right for standing on most of the time. The boy from Hill O'Beath turned the Rangers side from a good one into a great one. His finesse on a football field was really something to behold and it lifted the Light Blues' powerful, aggressive and penetrating type of game on to a different plane.

Suddenly, it was a case of 'By The Left' for Rangers – in more ways than one. Baxter quickly forged a brilliant left-wing partnership with Ralph Brand and Davie Wilson, but he was also conscripted to the Black Watch just after signing for Rangers. Happily, his square-bashing days rarely interrupted his career at Ibrox and the army were willing to co-operate with Rangers over the availability of their new star.

The season was the start of a wonderful period in the club's history. The

OFF TO WEST GERMANY The Rangers party get ready to fly to Moenchengladbach in 1960. In front are: Norrie Martin, Davie Wilson, John Greig, Billy Ritchie, Ralph Brand, Jimmy Millar, Bobby Shearer, Harry Davis and Bobby King. On the plane steps are: Scot Symon, John Lawrence, Ronnie McKinnon, Willie Penman, Alex Scott, Joe Craven, Max Murray, Ian McMillan and Willie Henderson.

JIM BAXTER The greatest of them all? Many would say so. It was £17,500 well spent in 1960 when Scot Symon brought 'Slim Jim' to Ibrox from Raith Rovers. An undoubted footballing genius, midfielder Baxter was the star of the brilliant 1960s team and he knew it. The fans adored him but his rebellious nature meant many missed training sessions, and sleepless nights for Scot Symon. Capped thirty-four times for Scotland, he left Ibrox in 1965 to join Sunderland for £72,500 and although he returned in 1969, it was only a temporary reprise and he retired the following year.

League Cup was the first piece of silverware collected. After overcoming Celtic in the qualifying section, Rangers stormed to Hampden where goals from Ralph Brand and Alex Scott saw off Kilmarnock.

Celtic had no answer to the Light Blues that season and the first League encounter summed up the supremacy Baxter was helping to instil over their 'Old Firm' rivals. A crowd of 40,000 watched Rangers win 5–1 at Parkhead – it was Celtic's heaviest home defeat for many a day. The New Year clash at Ibrox was far closer, but goals from Brand and Wilson earned a 2–1 win as Scot Symon's men marched towards a thirty-second championship triumph for the club.

Kilmarnock pursued them closely throughout and indeed picked up all four points from the matches between the sides. But an emphatic 7–3 win over Ayr United, Killie's neighbours, at Ibrox on the last day of the season was enough to give Rangers the title by a solitary point.

A crushing 5–2 win by Motherwell at Ibrox ended the hopes of a 'treble' and the Scottish Cup was relinquished. However, it was in the European Cup-Winners' Cup that Rangers caught the imagination of their fans and of footballing people all over Britain. No side from the United Kingdom had won a European trophy and the Light Blues were determined to be the first.

Rangers' intent was clear from the very first round when they faced highly-respected Hungarian team Ferencvaros. The 36,000 crowd at Ibrox got a shock in the first leg when a superb goal from Orosz gave the visitors a 1–0 lead at the interval, but their worries were wiped away in the second half. Harold Davis, a lionheart of a player, provided the equalizer and further goals from Jimmy Millar (two) and Ralph Brand earned a 4–2 lead to take to Hungary.

Ferencvaros took a 2–0 lead on their home soil to level the aggregate scores, but a sixty-first minute goal from Davie Wilson deservedly won the tie for Rangers.

There were no problems at all in the second round, which was surprising as the West German Cup-holders, Borussia Moenchengladbach, were expected to provide far stiffer opposition. A 3–0 win in Germany made the Ibrox leg no more than a formality, but Scot Symon demanded full effort from his players nonetheless and the supporters were rewarded with a stunning 8–0 victory in which Ralph Brand scored a hat-trick.

That took Rangers to the semi-finals and a 'Battle of Britain' clash with the marvellous Wolves side, a major force in England at the time. The men from Molineux had been crowned English champions twice in the previous three seasons and were installed by many bookmakers as favourites to win the Cup-Winners' Cup.

Rangers did not have their problems to seek and the first-leg match at Ibrox saw them line-up with central defender Doug Baillie, a £16,000 signing from Airdrie at the start of the season, wearing the number nine jersey. Regular first-teamer Jimmy Millar was side-lined with a back injury and Rangers' troubles worsened with just nine minutes of the match gone when Harold Davis suffered a leg injury. He limped sadly to outside-right for the remainder of the game with Davie Wilson switching to defence.

Not surprisingly, Wolves had the initiative and both Bobby Shearer and Eric Caldow made desperate goal-line clearances when keeper Billy Ritchie was beaten. Willed on by the bulk of the 80,000 crowd, Rangers snatched a first-half lead when Alex Scott gave Wolves and England star Ron Flowers the run-around before scoring with a terrific twenty-yard shot. It was all quite against the run of play and as the second half wore on, Rangers were happy to hold out against the furious Wolves onslaught. Astonishingly, though, a massive bonus came the way of the Light Blues six minutes from time when the Wolves defence gifted a second goal, eagerly accepted by Ralph Brand. It was extraordinary that Rangers should be taking a 2–0 lead to England for the return after Lady Luck had frowned upon them – but they now knew that a place in the final awaited them.

The game was played on 19 April, but Molineux was hazardous as heavy snow fell. As expected, Wolves attacked incessantly from the kick-off, but as the interval approached with Rangers having survived, they began to lose heart. The Ibrox men then delivered a killer blow right on half-time when Alex Scott opened the scoring and made the aggregate score 3–0. There was no way back for a deflated Wolves side and Broadbent's equalizer mid-way through the second half was merely a consolation.

So Rangers had become the first Scottish club to reach a European final and there they had to face the Italians of Fiorentina. It was a two-legged affair and once again Scot Symon had to prepare for the disadvantage of playing the home match first of all.

The Italians clearly possessed a lot of skilful players and Kurt Hamrin, their Swedish international winger, was renowned throughout Europe. Sadly, the capacity crowd at Ibrox had little chance to appreciate such a fine side. Fiorentina instead adopted the kind of tactics that have long given Italian football a bad name. Rangers were continually frustrated by the body-checking and all-round fouling perpetrated by their opponents and the referee never had control of the match.

The writing was on the wall in just eleven minutes when a poor pass-back from Harold Davis was pounced upon by left-winger Petris who set up his inside-forward Milan for a simple opening goal.

It was going to be one of those nights for Rangers and if they didn't realize it at that moment, they did six minutes later. A penalty-kick was awarded when Ian McMillan hit the turf after a challenge by Fiorentina skipper Orzan. Rangers skipper Eric Caldow stepped up to take the kick. As Caldow made his move towards the ball, keeper Albertosi rushed forward like a maniac and the surprised Ranger drove the ball wildly past. The referee refused to have the spot-kick retaken and Rangers night of frustration had well and truly set in.

Rangers tried desperately hard to equalize but could find no way through the often cynical defence, three of whom were booked. Instead, it was Fiorentina who scored again, a sickening blow for Rangers right on the final whistle as Milan dispossessed Bobby Shearer, exchanged passes with Hamrin and shot past the exposed Ritchie. The trip to Florence for the second leg now assumed the mantle of 'Mission Impossible'.

At least Rangers had the boost of Jimmy Millar's return from injury and his reputation clearly worried Fiorentina who deployed two men to mark the centre-forward. When Kurt Hamrin crossed for Milan to score his third goal of the final after just twelve minutes in the Florence Stadium, it all seemed immaterial. The Rangers players, though, displayed tremendous spirit and the partisan home crowd became less boisterous in the sixtieth minute when Alex Scott converted a low cross from Davie Wilson.

Urged on by the midfield promptings of Baxter and McMillan, Rangers were now the better side and the tireless Millar was unlucky not to add a second goal, which would have given them a fighting chance in the closing stages. Instead, it was the magnificent Kurt Hamrin who closed the final chapter of a memorable European campaign for Rangers. The Swede burst forward from midfield and from what seemed an impossible angle on the right, he drove a wickedly swerving shot past the despairing Billy Ritchie into the roof of the net. It was an ultimately disappointing end to a dramatic season, but the signs were clear that Scot Symon was assembling a side who could compete and win at the highest level.

The departure of Ian McColl came at the end of the term. The 34-year-old former captain of the club was hanging up his boots to take up his new position as Scotland's team manager. Others to move on were centre-half Willie Telfer and midfielder Sammy Baird.

The side who would achieve so much in the next few seasons had taken shape and looked like this as the 1961–62 season began: Billy Ritchie, Bobby Shearer, Eric Caldow, Harold Davis, Bill Paterson, Jim Baxter, Alex Scott, Ian McMillan, Jimmy Millar, Ralph Brand, Davie Wilson.

There was no shortage of young talent eager to make their mark, too. The reserve side won everything in sight that season and Willie Henderson and John Greig emerged to stake their claims for first-team places.

The championship was lost to a magnificent Dundee side who won 5–1 at Ibrox early in the season, striker Alan Gilzean scoring four of the goals. Rangers could still have retained their title, but for a slump at the end which saw them drop seven points in seven games to finish up trailing the Dens Park men by three points.

The supporters were appeased with the winning of both domestic cup competitions and Rangers had the satisfaction of eliminating Dundee from the League Cup in the qualifying stages. Hearts were the final opponents and the Edinburgh men were probably unlucky not to win the trophy at the first attempt, failing to make their pressure count in a 1–1 draw. Rangers made them pay and the replay saw a 3–1 win for the Ibrox men that didn't flatter them. The Scottish Cup was won in similarly stylish fashion, Ralph Brand and Davie Wilson scoring the goals in a 2–0 win over St Mirren witnessed by 126,930 fans at Hampden.

The European Cup campaign saw Rangers progress confidently to the quarter-finals, but a 4–1 defeat in Belgium by Standard Liege ended the story. The two eighteen-year-old starlets, Henderson and Greig, played in that first leg but neither were fielded for the second game at Ibrox. Ian McMillan returned from injury to reclaim his place from Greig, but Henderson's absence was less straightforward. The tiny winger was caught up in a traffic-jam on his way to the ground and arrived too late to play! Alex Scott pulled back on the number seven jersey and Rangers made a brave attempt to recover the deficit. In the end, their 2–0 win was appreciated by the 76,000 crowd but was in vain.

With two pots in the trophy room, it was a happy Rangers party who jetted off to Russia for an historic tour in the summer of 1962. Defender Greig was a revelation and firmly staked his claim for a regular place the next season and Henderson's wing wizardry delighted the Soviet fans. Lokomotiv Moscow and Dynamo Tbilisi were beaten and a 1–1 draw with Russian champions Dynamo Kiev completed a marvellously successful trip.

Rangers were greeted by thousands of supporters on the tarmac at Renfrew Airport on their return home and big things were expected from the team in 1962–63.

The players didn't disappoint their fans, the championship and Scottish Cup being collected by a team clearly superior to every other in Scotland at the time. Only two League games were lost and Rangers ended the season nine points ahead of their nearest challengers, Kilmarnock. Celtic were beaten home and away with the supporters particularly relishing the 4–0 triumph at Ibrox on New Year's Day.

Jimmy Millar thrived on the superb service he received from McMillan, Baxter, Henderson and Wilson, finishing top scorer with forty-five goals. Bill Paterson was given a free transfer and he was replaced with 22-year-old Ronnie McKinnon who quickly made the centre-half position his own. Rangers were still not the finished article and if the fans thought they were, the second round of the European Cup-Winners' Cup showed them otherwise as the Spurs side of Mackay, White and Greaves eliminated the Light Blues on an 8–4 aggregate.

The season ended on the highest possible note, though, with a Scottish Cup final triumph over Celtic. Heroics by keeper Frank Haffey defied the Ibrox men in a 1–1 draw, but the replay, witnessed by 120,263 fans, was quite one-sided in Rangers favour. Ian McMillan replaced £26,500 signing from St Mirren, George McLean, in midfield and his return brought the best out of Jim Baxter. The duo were the orchestrators of a magnificent ninety minutes and Celtic could offer little in the way of resistance. Ralph Brand scored a couple with Davie Wilson also hitting the target, but the 3–0 scoreline didn't convey Rangers' superiority.

The 1963–64 season began on a high note for Rangers supporters when Jim Baxter put pen to paper on a new contract. Things would get even better. Baxter had asked for a move but Scot Symon and new chairman John Lawrence – he had taken over in February following the sad death of John Wilson – managed to persuade their star player to remain.

The tragic leg-break of Eric Caldow in the 1962 England–Scotland international meant that Davie Provan began the season as regular left-back, while Jimmy Millar had a rival for his striker's role in the shape of young Jim Forrest.

Forrest couldn't have started off any better, scoring twice in a 3–0 League Cup win over Celtic at Parkhead and Rangers romped to the final. The new

RUSSIAN ROULETTE The Rangers
defence live dangerously during a match
against Locomotiv Moscow on their 1962
pioneering tour of Russia. John Greig, Billy
Ritchie and Bobby Shearer are the relieved
Rangers.

WILLIE HENDERSON Signed as a
schoolboy in 1960, Willie was a brilliant
right-winger and made his début for the
Rangers first team at the age of seventeen.
He achieved what many people thought to
be impossible in forcing Alex Scott out of
the team and he was a character much-loved
by the supporters. He eventually left in 1972
to join Sheffield Wednesday and gave the
Hillsborough club excellent service before
going on to play in Hong Kong. He was
capped twenty-nine times by Scotland.

WHAT A WELCOME Thousands of supporters crowd on to the tarmac at Renfrew Airport to welcome the successful Rangers squad back to Scotland after the Russian tour which caught the imagination of the public.

Left RONNIE MCKINNON Described early in his career as 'too small', Ronnie disproved that theory with fourteen years of marvellous service to Rangers after signing in 1959 from Dunipace Juniors. A calm, unassuming central defender, he was a vital member of the Ibrox side and won every domestic honour. He also won twenty-eight caps for Scotland.

Opposite BOBBY SHEARER A great Rangers captain, Bobby is held aloft by jubilant team-mates with the Scottish Cup after the 1963 replay success against Celtic. A brave and clever right-back, he was signed from Hamilton Accies in 1955 for £2,000 and stayed at Ibrox until 1965 when he joined Queen of the South as a player-coach. He won six League Championship medals with Rangers.

goalscoring sensation struck again at Hampden, scoring four times in the 5–0 triumph over Morton with his cousin, Alex Willoughby, grabbing the other.

The first cup of the season was in the Ibrox trophy-room and domestic glory was all that was left to go for after a first-round European Cup exit. The 7–0 aggregate defeat looked bad, but at the hands of Real Madrid – Puskas, Di Stefano, Gento and the rest – it was almost bearable. Anyhow, it was soon forgotten as Rangers swept majestically to their thirty-fourth League title, six points clear of the chasing pack.

Now only Dundee in the Scottish Cup final stood between Rangers and a repeat of the 'treble' they first achieved back in 1948–49. The Dens Park side had finished just sixth in the League table but were determined to spoil the party for the Rangers fans in the 120,982 crowd.

For a long time, it seemed as though the marvellous goalkeeping of Bert Slater would allow them to pull off a shock. He seemed unbeatable until the seventy-first minute when Jimmy Millar headed home a corner-kick from Willie Henderson. Astonishingly, right from the restart Dundee rushed upfield and equalized through Kenny Cameron. Rangers had been on top for so long and when they had finally broken through, Dundee's answer was immediate. Momentarily stunned, Rangers resumed the attack and with just a minute to go they dramatically regained the lead. Again Henderson provided the centre, again Millar supplied the headed finish. It was a personal triumph for Millar, having regained his place at the end of the season, and Ralph Brand's goal on the final whistle merely helped confirm Rangers superiority. Thus ended a glorious season which Rangers would not see the like of again for a long time.

Not surprisingly, they found it difficult to follow in 1964–65, but the loss of two of the trophies was a major blow. The Ibrox men could finish just fifth in the championship table, six points behind winners Kilmarnock and their Scottish Cup hopes were extinguished by Hibs in the third round. The League Cup, at least, was retained with Jim Forrest again finding the competition to his liking. He scored both goals in the 2–1 final win over Celtic.

It was the only silver lining in a cloudy season. Rangers suffered a dreadful blow in the European Cup when Jim Baxter broke his right leg in the final minute of a superb 2–0 win over Rapid Vienna in Austria in which he had been the outstanding player. His absence in the next round against Inter Milan was critical. Jim Forrest's away goal in the San Siro gave hope for the return, but 3–1 was enough for the Italians who, despite Forrest scoring again at Ibrox, went on to win the European Cup. Forrest scored an amazing fifty-seven goals in the course of the season and it was unfortunate for him that Rangers' failure to repeat the previous season's success took some of the shine off his achievement.

It was all-change time again. Ian McMillan departed, back to Airdrie for £5,000, and Bobby Shearer was given a free transfer after a ten-year career that saw him play 431 first-team games. The most savage blow for the fans, though, was the transfer of Baxter, their idol, to Sunderland for £72,500 on 25 May 1965. Danish international full-back Kai Johansen was snapped up from Morton for £20,000 as Scot Symon sought an infusion of new blood and another 'old hand' departed on the eve of the 1965–66 season, Ralph Brand signing for Manchester City in a £30,000 deal. Rangers now had to face up to a far more potent challenge from Celtic. Their 'Old Firm' rivals were now under the leadership of Jock Stein and emerging from the considerable doldrums they had been in. The Parkhead men underlined their intent with a 2–1 win over Rangers in the League Cup final and after a titanic struggle, it was Celtic who lifted the championship, their first since 1954, by a two-point margin.

Rangers were left to seek consolation in the Scottish Cup and were certainly not favourites in the 'Old Firm' final. They surprised many by holding ebullient Celtic to a goalless draw at Hampden. The replay caused an even bigger shock. Inspired by Scotland's Player of the Year, John Greig, Rangers displayed tremendous spirit and a superb twenty-five-yard rocket from Kai Johansen provided the only goal of the game and gave the Light Blues their nineteenth Scottish Cup success. That gave them passage into the European Cup-Winners' Cup in 1966–67, an amazing season memorable for several reasons.

Rangers contrived to save their best form for the European ties and Glentoran and Borussia Dortmund were knocked out before a toss of a coin from skipper John Greig gave them the verdict over Real Zaragoza. Slavia Sofia were beaten both in Bulgaria and at Ibrox by 1–0 to put Rangers into a European final for the second time. However, it was not enough simply to get there on this occasion, as Celtic had equalled the feat in the European Cup, and just six days before Rangers were to play Bayern Munich in the Nuremberg final, Jock Stein's side had lifted the trophy with a 2–1 win over Inter Milan.

There is no doubt that this put added pressure on the Light Blues, but in all truth they would have overcome the West Germans had they had an accomplished finisher in their side on the night. Roger Hynd allowed Sepp Maier to make a save from a shot from the six-yard line and had that gone in, Rangers would have lifted the trophy. There were no goals when the whistle blew at the end of ninety minutes and despite the inspirational urgings of John Greig in extra-time, no Ranger could find a way past Franz Beckenbauer and his colleagues. Four minutes into the second period of extra-time, Helmut Roth directed the ball past the despairing Norrie Martin in Rangers' goal and the chance of glory had gone.

It was a dreadfully discouraging end to a season which would be best forgotten, but never will be. That's because of 27 January 1967. Berwick Rangers 1, Rangers 0. That was the scoreline which rocked Scottish football as the Ibrox men crashed out of the Scottish Cup to the Second Division minnows. It was the end of the Ibrox line for Jim Forrest and George McLean, blamed somewhat cruelly for the disastrous exit. Soon afterwards, Forrest signed for Preston North End and McLean went to Dundee in a deal that brought Andy Penman to Rangers. Jimmy Millar was given a free transfer and Scot Symon took on a new assistant in the shape of Clyde manager Davie White.

In the space of just four seasons, Rangers had gone from all-conquering heroes to living in the shadow of Celtic who had won every trophy available in 1966–67. The fans wanted success in Europe to equal the achievement of their greatest rivals. They would have to wait a little bit longer.

Opposite above   OUR NAME GOES HERE   Scot Symon points out the place on the Scottish Cup plinth to Willie Henderson, Harold Davis, Davie Wilson and Ian McMillan after the 1962 triumph against St Mirren.

Opposite below   ERIC CALDOW   One of the greatest left-backs the game has seen, Eric was signed from Muirkirk Juniors in 1952 and spent fourteen successful years as a Rangers and Scotland star. He started as many attacks for his own side as he stopped the opposition's, and his total of forty caps would have been greater but for the broken leg he sustained at Wembley in 1963. He won five League Championship, two Scottish Cup and three League Cup winners medals.

Above   KAI'S CRACKER   One of the most famous goals in Rangers history. It's the Scottish Cup final replay of 1966 and Kai Johansen, the club's Danish full-back, has struck a fearsome drive past the despairing reach of Ronnie Simpson to give Rangers an unexpected 1–0 win.

6
Triumph in Europe

No one could possibly have anticipated the drama that would take place at Ibrox just five months after they had come so close to glory in Europe. The dismissal of manager Scot Symon on 1 November 1967 shook Scottish football to the core. It came on the day that Celtic were playing in the World Club Championship match in South America and there's no doubt that there was envy of the Parkhead club both in the boardroom and on the terraces at Ibrox. The challenge had to be met and Rangers decided drastic action was the only course open to them. Nevertheless, with the team sitting proudly at the top of the League table at the time, it was still an astonishing blow for Symon to be dealt.

In thirteen years at the helm, he had taken Rangers to six League Championships, five Scottish Cup wins and four League Cup successes. The club had been the first in Scotland to reach a European final and Symon had taken them there twice. In the end, Celtic's day of glory in Lisbon was enough to end it all and Davie White was installed as the new manager of Rangers.

White had joined the club on 28 June that year, 1967, as assistant to Symon after having some success in charge of unfashionable Clyde. Symon accepted his departure from Ibrox with supreme grace and dignity, saying: 'Davie White is a very fine man. I wish him all the best. He is with a wonderful club.'

White took control of a side who had been eliminated by Celtic in the qualifying stages of the League Cup earlier in the season but who, after eight matches, were undefeated and leading the championship chase. Danish international goalkeeper Erik Sorensen had been signed from Morton and his arrival signalled the departure of Billy Ritchie to Partick Thistle. With scapegoats of the Berwick disaster, George McLean and Jim Forrest, gone it was Alex Ferguson who carried the responsibility of putting the ball in the back of the net. He was signed from Dunfermline Athletic for £65,000 and his first season was a success as he topped the scoring charts with a tally of twenty-four. Two great Rangers left the club – Jimmy Millar joined Dundee United with his free transfer and Davie Wilson also moved to Tannadice. Wilson's

Right LOOKING ON Ronnie McKinnon, ruled out of the 1972 Cup-Winners' Cup final, is flanked by John Lawrence and Matt Taylor as they watch Rangers train in the Nou Camp Stadium.

Left ALEX FERGUSON Now a famous figure in management, Fergie was signed by Rangers in 1967 for £65,000 from Dunfermline and proved a useful striker, scoring twenty-four goals in his first season. The emergence of Colin Stein, though, cut short his Ibrox career and he was sold to Falkirk for £20,000 in November 1969.

Below WILLIE JOHNSTON A left-winger who could also play in a more central striking role, 'Bud' joined Rangers as a sixteen-year-old in 1962 and soon established himself as an Ibrox hero. His pace over forty yards was amazing and he could cross the ball with consistent accuracy. Unfortunately rebellious, he was an entertainer and there was much sorrow when he joined West Bromwich Albion in 1972. He returned to Ibrox in 1980 and spent another two years with the club.

place in the side had been taken by exciting youngster Willie Johnston, but the left-wing role was then assumed by Orjan Persson. The Swedish star came to Ibrox from Dundee United in the deal that involved Wilson and midfielder Wilson Wood leaving the Light Blues.

When White took over the reins, Rangers were already safely through the first round of the Fairs Cup, a dramatic late goal from John Greig beating Dynamo Dresden 3–2 on aggregate. A week into the job, White had to prepare his men for the challenge of Cologne in the second round.

The first leg was at Ibrox and Rangers didn't let the 54,000 crowd down as their pressure on the West Germans' goal finally paid off in the second half. Alex Ferguson opened the scoring, Willie Henderson made it 2–0 and a quite brilliant header from Ferguson gave Rangers what looked like a comfortable cushion to take with them to Germany.

However, Cologne rocked the Ibrox men when Wolfgang Overath scored just thirty seconds into the match and two goals in the space of four second-half minutes levelled the aggregate score. The Germans had seized the initiative without question, but Rangers displayed magnificent courage and spirit in extra-time with Willie Henderson grabbing the goal which took them to the quarter-final.

At that stage, they met their match in the shape of Don Revie's emerging Leeds United side. Inspired by Billy Bremner, the Elland Road side forced a goalless draw in front of 80,000 fans at Ibrox and on their home patch they were just too good for Rangers, goals from Johnny Giles and Peter Lorimer ending Davie White's hopes of immediate glory.

By the time of that Fairs Cup exit, Hearts had knocked Rangers out of the Scottish Cup, but they were still hotly chasing the championship.

They were unbeaten but astonishingly even that wasn't good enough to stop Celtic retaining their title, even though Rangers took three points from the two 'Old Firm' clashes. The loss at Ibrox was the only one the Parkhead side suffered and on the last day of the season, Rangers went down 3–2 at home to Aberdeen and their faint hopes of pipping Celtic at the post were dashed.

White remained convinced his side were as good as Celtic and despite two defeats at the hands of their rivals in the League Cup section ties at the start of 1968–69, Rangers were confident of going one better in the championship this time around. A tremendous 4–2 win at Parkhead, with Willie Johnston scoring twice, in the second League match of the season certainly bore out the general optimism.

White still hadn't made any major signings but he put that to rights in some style on 31 October when he paid a Scottish record fee of £100,000 for Hibs striker Colin Stein. Remarkably, Stein scored hat-tricks in his first two games, 5–1 and 6–1 defeats of Arbroath and Hibs respectively – Rangers looked to be on the march.

Having beaten Vojvodina of Yugoslavia 2–1 on aggregate in the first round of the Fairs Cup, Stein was signed in time to chip in with two goals in the 9–1 aggregate destruction of Irish club Dundalk in round two.

The side was further strengthened by the arrival of tenacious midfielder Alex

COLIN STEIN   An Ibrox idol, Stein was a prolific scorer in his two spells with Rangers. His most famous goal was the header at Easter Road in 1975 which won the championship and ended Celtic's nine-year stranglehold on the title.

Opposite ANDY PENMAN A schoolboy prodigy, Andy was signed by Rangers from Dundee for £35,000 plus George McLean in 1967. A superb passer of the ball, he was a star of Rangers midfield until leaving to join Arbroath in 1973.

Above FRIENDLY ENEMIES Tom Forsyth tackles Rangers captain John Greig during a Motherwell–Rangers match in the early 1970s. Forsyth would later team up at Ibrox with Greig as part of a formidable Rangers side.

Right ALEX MACDONALD David White completed a great piece of business when he bought MacDonald from St Johnstone for £50,000 in 1968. A tenacious midfielder, he had seemingly limitless reserves of strength and stamina. A vital member of the European Cup-Winners' Cup winning side, 'Doddie' won three League Championship, four Scottish Cup and three League Cup winners medals with Rangers before joining Hearts for £30,000 in 1980.

MacDonald from St Johnstone for £50,000, but inconsistency was costing Rangers precious points in the title race. The arrival of the New Year saw them trailing leaders Celtic by five points and drawn games against opposition they were expected to defeat easily had contributed to that. A John Greig penalty-kick at Ibrox on 2 January reduced the deficit, the only goal of an 'Old Firm' game Rangers certainly deserved to win. The bad news from the game came in the shape of twenty-four people being taken to hospital injured after a crash barrier gave way on a stairway.

January brought smiles to Ibrox, though, when DWS Amsterdam were beaten home and away in the Fairs Cup to take Rangers into the quarter-finals. Their domestic cause was hardly helped, however, when Willie Johnston and Colin Stein were handed suspensions of three and four weeks respectively for ordering-offs received in League matches that month. Stein was sent-off again against Clyde in March – he also scored a hat-trick in the game! – and was banned until the end of the season. He had scored thirteen goals in eighteen League matches for the club and was badly missed as the championship challenge crumbled sadly in the closing weeks of the season, Rangers finishing up five points behind winners Celtic.

Progress in the Fairs and Scottish Cups at least kept the fans hopeful of some glory and 63,000 of them were at Ibrox in mid-March to see Athletico Bilbao provide the opposition. Rangers led just 2–1 until the final three minutes of the game when substitute Orjan Persson swung the game decisively in their favour. The Swede scored one goal and created another for Colin Stein to make the final scoreline far more convincing and give Rangers genuine optimism for the second leg in Spain.

The game was packed with drama, Estefano scoring in ten minutes and then Ibanez making it 2–0 nine minutes into the second half, leaving the Spaniards just one behind on aggregate. Rangers were under the cosh in the closing stages and both sides were reduced to ten men when Bilbao right-back Betzeun and Willie Johnston clashed violently. Nevertheless, Davie White's men held out and had booked their place in the semi-finals.

In between the two games against the Spaniards, Rangers had clinched their place in the Scottish Cup final with a scintillating semi-final performance against Aberdeen at Parkhead. Willie Henderson and Andy Penman were magnificent on the right flank, with Willie Johnston and Orjan Persson even better on the left. Aberdeen couldn't cope and lost 6–1 with ex-Rangers striker Jim Forrest grabbing their goal.

The final was against Celtic and despite Jock Stein's side having been crowned champions again, Rangers had beaten them twice in the League and approached the match with confidence. The ninety minutes, though, were a complete disaster for the men in light blue from the moment Billy McNeill gave Celtic a second-minute lead. It was sheer torture for the Rangers fans in the 132,870 crowd, and further goals from Bobby Lennox, George Connelly and Steve Chalmers didn't flatter Celtic – they were miles ahead. It was hardly the stuff to put the Ibrox men in the right frame of mind for their Fairs Cup semi-final matches against Newcastle United.

Rangers received superb backing from the 70,000 crowd at Ibrox for the first leg but, despite creating plenty of good chances against a very defensive Newcastle side, the game finished goalless and tipped the balance in favour of the Geordies. Rangers were left rueing a thirty-fourth-minute penalty-kick awarded when Willie McFaul fouled Orjan Persson, only for Andy Penman to see his effort from the spot saved by the United keeper.

Newcastle put the accent firmly on attack at St James' Park and although Rangers were not disgraced, nor did they ever look likely to cause an upset and grab an away win. The home side won 2–0, both goals scored in the second half by Scottish players – John Scott and Jackie Sinclair.

Rangers' season was over but their name was never away from the back pages in the close season as Davie White wielded the big stick and gave the headline writers plenty to think about. The biggest sensation came seven days after the Fairs Cup exit when Jim Baxter rejoined the club. He had been given a free transfer by Nottingham Forest and a £10,000 signing-on fee secured his services to the Ibrox cause once more. Out went Alex Willoughby to Aberdeen for £25,000, Roger Hynd to Crystal Palace for £25,000 and Alex Smith to Aberdeen for £25,000.

White knew that 1969–70 would be a crucial one for the club and was pinning his hopes on the return of the fans' idol, Baxter, to achieve the success they craved. His team wasn't short of talent. Ronnie McKinnon was as good a centre-half as any in the country while John Greig was a captain without peer. Sandy Jardine had matured into a class performer since his introduction in 1967, Colin Stein was a proven goalscorer and Willie Johnston was a real crowd-pleaser with intricate skills. The fluency and consistency of every successful side was what White was looking for and the added demands of producing the goods on the European stage put him under further pressure.

Things started off well enough. Rangers came from behind at Ibrox to beat Celtic 2–1 in their League Cup sectional tie. Jim Baxter was superb while Orjan Persson and Willie Johnston got the goals that mattered. That form couldn't be maintained, though, and a mistake by goalkeeper Gerry Neef a week later at Parkhead allowed Celtic to take revenge with a 1–0 win, Tommy Gemmell doing the damage after Neef fumbled a Bobby Murdoch free-kick. A dropped point at home to Raith Rovers ended the League Cup interest and for the third season in a row Rangers had lost out in the sectional stage to Celtic.

Worse was to come as Rangers League form failed to achieve anything like the consistency they needed to dislodge Celtic from the top spot in Scotland. A Harry Hood goal gave Jock Stein's side a 1–0 win, their first League victory at Ibrox for twelve years, in mid-September and in some places the knives were out for Davie White. He gained respite from the first round of the European Cup-Winners' Cup. Two goals from Willie Johnston defeated Steaua Bucharest at Ibrox and a highly disciplined display in Rumania earned a goalless draw to take Rangers through.

Rangers travelled to Poland for the second round and the seeds were sown for White's demise when Gornik Zabrze won the first leg behind the Iron Curtain 3–1. Five days later, White sold striker Alex Ferguson to Falkirk for

SWEET SIXTEEN   A goal of Ibrox folklore. Derek Johnstone, just sixteen-years-old, rises between Billy McNeill and Jim Craig to head the only goal of the 1970 League Cup final against Celtic to give Rangers a 1–0 win and their first trophy in four years.

CONGRATULATIONS   Disappointment is etched on the face of Colin Stein as he shakes hands with Sepp Maier and Gerd Muller after Rangers' Fairs Cup defeat at the hands of Bayern Munich in 1970–71. Stein would be smiling in Europe the following season.

RONNIE'S BIG DAY   Ronnie McKinnon, depu-
tizing as captain for the injured John Greig, lifts the
League Cup aloft after the 1970 success.

HORROR   The twisted barriers of Stairway 13 at Ibrox
as officials inspect the scene after the second disaster
to befall the stadium. Sixty-six people were killed at the
end of the 'Old Firm' meeting on 2 January 1971.

£20,000 and it would be one of his last decisions as manager of Rangers Football Club.

The team gave 63,000 fans false hope in the eighteenth minute of the return leg against Gornik at Ibrox when Jim Baxter scored a superb goal. Another one and Rangers would be level but all of a sudden the Poles stepped up a gear. Olek made it 1–1 on the night and two goals from the brilliant Lubanski and then Skowronek made the final aggregate 6–2 for a side who went on to reach the final.

The next day, 27 November, Rangers announced the dismissal of Davie White. The desperately sought-for success in Europe was still just an ambition and the board wanted something to be done about it. While Willie Thornton took temporary charge, chairman John Lawrence lined up the man he wanted as manager. In early December, he shook hands at the front door of Ibrox with Willie Waddell.

One of the club's legends as a player was back, this time in the manager's office from where he would have to take Rangers out of the doldrums to a position where they could meet the challenge being thrown down by Celtic.

Despite a good start, there would be no miracles produced by Waddell. The Scottish Cup campaign was ended by a 3–1 defeat at Parkhead in February, and winning just two of their last ten League matches ensured that Rangers were runners-up to Celtic again – this time by a massive twelve points.

Waddell went through the playing-staff like a bulldozer, starting at the back where he recruited a new goalkeeper. Peter McCloy was signed from Motherwell in a swap deal which took Bobby Watson and Brian Heron to Fir Park. Jim Baxter, Norrie Martin, Erik Sorensen and Davie Provan were among those given free transfers, Denis Setterington was sold to Falkirk for £10,000 and Orjan Persson was put up for sale. The new boss also brought in his own coaching team. Jock Wallace was recruited as his number two from Hearts while former Rangers player Stan Anderson was snapped up from Clyde to become assistant trainer. Orjan Persson was sold, back to Orgryte in Sweden for a minimal fee and Waddell laid down the law to his players – he wanted success and he wanted it quickly.

Rangers began the 1970–71 season with a 4–1 win over Dunfermline in the League Cup and stormed through their qualifying section unbeaten, giving the fans some cause for optimism. The first 'Old Firm' match of the season put things in perspective, though, goals from Hughes and Murdoch giving Celtic a 2–0 win at Parkhead and emphasizing how far Rangers had to progress.

While he was always on the lookout in the transfer market, Waddell was also searching for young players to break through at Ibrox and a week after that defeat by Celtic, a significant first-team début was made. Striker Derek Johnstone was just sixteen-years-old when he lined up in front of 30,000 Ibrox fans against Cowdenbeath. The tall kid made an instant impact, scoring twice in a 5–0 win. It was the prelude to a real fairytale for Johnstone and Rangers, but not before they had made a contentious exit from Europe.

The Light Blues were superb in West Germany in the first leg of their Fairs Cup tie against Bayern Munich and had they taken their chances, would have had the outcome sewn up before flying back to Glasgow. As it was, a series of pieces of bad luck and fine goalkeeping from the brilliant Sepp Maier denied them, and a wonderfully taken goal from Franz Beckenbauer gave Bayern a scarcely credible 1–0 win.

Rangers piled on the pressure in the return at Ibrox in front of an 83,000 crowd who willed an equalizer throughout – but it was the Germans who scored again. The home side bitterly protested that the Swiss referee had awarded an indirect free-kick when Ronnie McKinnon fouled Gerd Muller at the edge of the penalty-area, but Muller's swerving shot that beat Peter McCloy was allowed to stand. That blow came in the eightieth minute and amazingly Rangers equalized a minute later through Colin Stein. Their European ambitions were over already nonetheless.

The supporters' minds were taken away from that disappointment as Rangers reached the League Cup final with a 6–2 aggregate win over Hibernian in the quarter-final and a 2–0 victory against Cowdenbeath in the semi-final at Hampden.

Preparation for the final could hardly have been worse. Celtic were already favourites for the game, even before inspirational skipper John Greig was ruled out of the Rangers side through injury. The knock was sustained as Waddell's men crashed 2–0 at home to Aberdeen on 17 October 1970 to go three points adrift of League leaders Celtic, a week before the big Hampden date. Boss Waddell took the gamble of playing sixteen-year-old Derek Johnstone in the match with Alfie Conn drafted in to wear Greig's number four jersey.

The Rangers fans in the 106,263 crowd could never have imagined the drama that would unfold before their eyes. The Ibrox players threw the formbook out of the window and fully deserved to win their first trophy since lifting the Scottish Cup back in 1966. There was only one goal scored – but what a goal to savour, particularly for the scorer, Derek Johnstone. Willie Henderson began the move and Alex MacDonald's pass set Willie Johnston scampering down the right. His cross was a beauty and the Rangers fans gasped as Johnstone rose magnificently between the experienced duo of Billy McNeill and Jim Craig to power an unstoppable header past Evan Williams. Ronnie McKinnon collected the trophy and the jubilant Rangers supporters were convinced that the good times were back. It wasn't quite that straightforward.

As Rangers failed to make any significant challenge to Celtic at the top of the League, 2 January 1971 arrived to make everyone forget about football. At the end of the 'Old Firm' clash at Ibrox, the steel barriers on Stairway 13 in the ground gave way and a total of sixty-six people were suffocated to death and many more injured in the resulting crush. It was thought that Colin Stein's dramatic equalizer for Rangers in the final seconds of the match, a minute after Jimmy Johnstone had opened the scoring for Celtic, caused fans who were leaving the ground to come back and meet a wave of jubilant fans coming in the opposite direction. The enquiry that followed the horrific disaster found this to be untrue. The crowd had remained to the end and were heading in the same direction when the crush took place halfway down Stairway 13. The game had been good-natured and there were just two arrests made by police, both for drunkenness, in the all-ticket crowd of 80,000.

The 'Old Firm' came together to help the victims of the tragedy and a special match between Scotland and a Rangers and Celtic Select XI was played in front of an 81,405 crowd at Hampden.

The remainder of the season was overshadowed by the devastating disaster. Rangers trailed a poor fourth behind Celtic in the League table and suffered bad injuries to Dave Smith and Sandy Jardine, both breaking a leg.

Rangers did have the chance to end the season on a high note as they reached the Scottish Cup final. Again the opponents were Celtic. The Parkhead men looked every inch favourites in the first half and Bobby Lennox gave them the lead in the fortieth minute. Rangers threw on Derek Johnstone in place of Andy Penman in the final twenty minutes and the teenager made it 'Roy of the Rovers' all over again when he headed the equalizer with just three minutes left.

It earned a replay for which Rangers were without Alex Miller, victim of a broken cheekbone in the first match. Willie Waddell drafted in 21-year-old Jim Denny to make his début in the match. The youngster, only recently snapped up from junior football, performed admirably but could do little as goals from Lou Macari and Harry Hood inside two first-half minutes set Celtic on their way to victory. An own goal from Jim Craig in the fifty-eighth minute gave the Light Blues hope, but it proved false and the Parkhead men lifted the trophy.

Willie Waddell began to pick up the pieces. Kai Johansen was handed a free transfer and in the close season the manager made a significant signing when he brought winger Tommy McLean to Ibrox from Kilmarnock for £60,000.

The 1971–72 season will always shine out for Rangers and their fans whenever the club's history is spoken of or written about. Yet, it all began so inauspiciously. Drawn against Celtic in the qualifying section of the League Cup, Rangers lost both games, 2–0 and 3–0, at Ibrox – Parkhead was undergoing construction work. Celtic also won the first League encounter and Rangers' form in the championship was as inconsistent as ever. When the New Year arrived they were seven points adrift of their old rivals at the top of the League. With this in mind, it was a blessed relief for the team's supporters as they watched Rangers leave their domestic form behind them when they stepped into the European arena.

In the first round of the European Cup-Winners' Cup, they faced the stylish French side Rennes. The first leg was away from home and Rangers were given the perfect start to their European campaign when Willie Johnston opened the scoring in the sixty-eighth minute. Substitute Redon equalized for Rennes ten minutes later, but the 1–1 draw was a good scoreline to take back to Glasgow. A crowd of 40,000 watched the second leg and Rangers fully deserved the victory given to them by the only goal of the game, scored by Alex MacDonald in the first half.

The second round paired Willie Waddell's men with the formidable Portuguese Cup-holders, Sporting Lisbon, and the two games produced incessant thrills and drama.

Great shakes The legendary Franz Beckenbauer shakes hands with Dave Smith before the start of the 1971–72 Cup-Winners' Cup semi-final between Rangers and Bayern Munich. Signed from Aberdeen for £40,000 in 1966, Smith was a terrific half-back who deputized for the injured John Greig during part of that famous season.

Tommy McLean A tactically aware right-sided attacker, McLean was a great servant to Rangers after signing from Kilmarnock for £60,000 in 1971. He won three League Championships, five Scottish Cup and two League Cup winners medals in addition to his part in the 1972 European triumph.

The first leg was watched by 50,000 at Ibrox and the crowd saw Rangers race to a 3–0 interval lead while producing some sparkling football. Colin Stein scored twice and Willie Henderson grabbed the other as Sporting wondered what had hit them. If the Rangers fans thought it was all over, they got just as much of a shock as the players did when the Portuguese side stormed back into the tie. Chic and Gomes – the latter scoring four minutes from the end – found the net to make the second leg look much, much tougher.

No one could have scripted the drama that unfolded in the second game, watched by 60,000 fans in Lisbon. Yazalde gave Sporting the lead in the twenty-sixth minute to level the aggregate score, only for Colin Stein to net for Rangers just sixty seconds later. The home side went in ahead at the interval thanks to Tome's goal in the thirty-seventh minute, but Stein and Rangers wouldn't be denied and it was Colin who made it 2–2 on the night with a goal in the first minute of the second half. That would have been enough to take Rangers through but Gomes forced extra-time when he made it 3–2 for Sporting on the night and 5–5 on aggregate with his goal seven minutes from the end of the regulation ninety minutes.

In the tenth minute of a nerve-wracking extra period, Willie Henderson scored for Rangers – surely they could hold on now. The amazing sequence of events continued, though, when Perez levelled the overall scores. That was how it finished up – 4–3 on the night to Sporting, 6–6 on aggregate with Rangers having scored more away goals. That, they thought, would take them through. The referee, though, ruled differently and the teams were told a penalty shoot-out was required to decide who would go into the third-round draw. The Rangers players seemed to accept that away goals in extra-time didn't count – this was the referee's line of thought. The spot-kicks were taken, Rangers lost out and seemed to be out of Europe. But the drama would go on after the final whistle. Journalist John Fairgrieve, sadly no longer with us, rushed from the press box and managed to get into the Rangers dressing-room. There he waved a UEFA rulebook at Willie Waddell and told the stunned Rangers boss that his side had won – away goals *did* count as double in extra-time! The UEFA representative at the match was sought out and after some delay, it was officially noted that Rangers had won.

Waddell didn't know whether to laugh or cry, having lost key defender Ronnie McKinnon in the match with a double fracture of the right leg. By the time the quarter-final came around in March of 1972, he didn't have to worry. Dave Smith had returned from his serious leg-break and was performing brilliantly in McKinnon's place.

Italian giants Torino stood between Rangers and a place in the last four and the Ibrox men travelled to the Communale Stadium for the first leg. Again, Waddell had his men superbly briefed and in confident mood and they produced another splendid display on foreign soil. They got off to a dream start when Willie Johnston scored in the twelfth minute, driving the ball home after keeper Castellini had failed to hold a great cross from Willie Mathieson. The disciplined tactics of the Ibrox men frustrated both the Italian players and the crowd of 35,000, but Torino did snatch an equalizer in the sixty-first minute,

INTO GLORY John Greig leads Rangers on to the pitch at the Nou Camp Stadium in Barcelona on 24 May 1972 for the European Cup-Winners' Cup final against Moscow Dynamo.

LAP OF HONOUR The Rangers players show off the European Cup-Winners' Cup at Ibrox on their return from Barcelona.

Pulici netting a scrappy goal after Peter McCloy and Colin Jackson had blocked efforts on the line.

There were 75,000 packed into Ibrox for the return leg and they saw Rangers put Torino under pressure right from the start. Frustration was beginning to set in when half-time arrived with the score-sheet still blank, but the first minute of the second half saw Rangers grab the only goal of the game. Tommy McLean, already proving to be a superb buy, sprinted clear down the right and sent over a dangerous cross. Willie Johnston headed the ball down and the Italian defence were in disarray as Alex MacDonald slotted the ball over the line.

Rangers were in the semi-finals and the draw paired them with old rivals Bayern Munich. After defeat at the hands of the West Germans in the 1967 Final and again in the 1970–71 Fairs Cup, revenge was an extra incentive for the players.

Again, Rangers enjoyed the benefit of the first leg being away from home and in front of 40,000 fans in Munich, they even bettered their previous performances on the Continent that season. Bayern never looked happy against a hustling, confident and skilful Rangers side. Gerd Muller was marked magnificently by Colin Jackson, while Dave Smith and Derek Johnstone were almost impenetrable at the centre of the defence. Rangers refused to lose their cool when the home side opened the scoring in the twenty-third minute through Paul Breitner. They remained patient and were rewarded with a forty-ninth-minute equalizer. Colin Stein dragged the ball wide of Sepp Maier and when he drove across the face of the goal, midfielder Zobel headed into his own net. It was no more than Rangers deserved from a match they could easily have won and they were highly confident of success at Ibrox.

Rangers were dealt a blow, however, when skipper John Greig limped from the field in agony after thirty minutes of the Scottish Cup semi-final against Hibs at Hampden just four days before the game. Derek Parlane was called up for his European début as Willie Waddell shuffled his pack – and came up trumps.

Bayern were totally shocked as Rangers scored in the very first minute of the second leg to the delight of the 80,000 crowd. Sandy Jardine got the goal with a left-foot shot that Maier assumed was going wide. The West Germans looked a beaten side from that moment on while the Light Blues oozed confidence. Young Parlane capped his glory night when he made it 2–0 in the twenty-third minute, smashing home a Willie Johnston corner. That was the emphatic moment and Rangers had booked their place in the Nou Camp Stadium, Barcelona, to face Russian aces Moscow Dynamo in the European Cup-Winners' Cup final.

Rangers' domestic form continued to disappoint and they made an exit from the Scottish Cup when Hibs won the semi-final replay 2–0 with something to spare. Furthermore, only 3,000 fans bothered to turn up at Ibrox for the final League match of the season, a 4–2 win over Ayr United that confirmed third place in the table, sixteen points behind champions Celtic.

Dave Smith was deservedly named as Scotland's 'Player of the Year' and he would be a key man for Rangers in the final. Willie Waddell had injury worries, though, about John Greig and Colin Jackson. Greig recovered in time to lead the team out on 24 May, but it was agony for Jackson who couldn't recover from his ankle injury in time.

Cheered on by 20,000 Rangers fans in the crowd of 35,000, these were the players who lined up for the final: Peter McCloy, Sandy Jardine, Willie Mathieson, John Greig, Derek Johnstone, Dave Smith, Tommy McLean, Alfie Conn, Colin Stein, Alex MacDonald, Willie Johnston.

Smith was the outstanding player on the field as Rangers took an immediate grip of the final and by half-time it looked all over. In the twenty-fourth minute, Colin Stein ran on to a great through ball from Smith and his rising shot flew past the helpless figure of keeper Pilgui into the roof of the net. Five minutes from the interval, Rangers made it 2–0 with Dave Smith again the creator. This time his deft chip caught the Dynamo defence square and Willie Johnston headed home. Even the Light Blues players could have been forgiven for thinking the cup was theirs when they scored a third goal four minutes into the second half. A massive kick-out from Peter McCloy fell kindly to Willie Johnston who gleefully slotted the ball past the devastated Pilgui.

Russian coach Konstantin Beskov had one last ace up his sleeve and threw on substitute Eschtrekov after the goal. Ten minutes later, the new player pulled one back and breathed fresh life into the tired Moscow side. The Rangers defence had to perform heroics as the Russians searched for another two goals – they got one, making it 3–2 with three minutes to go, thanks to Makovikov. The Ibrox men survived, though, and had achieved the prized ambition of winning a European trophy. It was a magnificent achievement, but one which was tragically sullied by the after-match events.

Thousands of delirious Rangers fans poured on to the pitch to celebrate, but were soon caught up in fights with worried and panic-stricken Spanish police wielding batons. The European Cup-Winners' Cup had to be presented to John Greig in a small room inside the dressing-room area, which was the saddest part of the whole affair. If anyone deserved the ultimate moment of glory, it was Greig. The repercussions from UEFA were severe. They banned Rangers from Europe for two seasons, to the dismay of everyone at the club. Chairman John Lawrence summed it up when he said: 'It has taken a lifetime to achieve success in Europe. Now it has all been thrown away for two years.'

Willie Waddell had no time to bask in the European glory and another of the old guard, Willie Henderson, was handed a free transfer. The biggest bombshell of the season, though, came on 7 June when Waddell announced he was resigning as manager of Rangers. He would become general manager while Jock Wallace was to take over as the new boss. It was a stunning move but Waddell was confident that Wallace was the man to take Rangers to greater glory. The former sergeant-major, who had played in goal for Berwick Rangers when they defeated Rangers in the Scottish Cup tie of 1967, had one target – to regain the championship. The title had last rested at Ibrox in 1964 – would Wallace be the one to end the famine?

HEAD MAN   Willie Johnston makes it 2–0 for Rangers in the Nou Camp Stadium and the Russians are left reeling with five minutes still left of the first half.

Opposite   below ALL   TOO MUCH   The emotion of winning the Cup-Winners' Cup gets to skipper John Greig and he breaks down in tears in the dressing-room after the historic match.

Above HERE WE GO Rangers
are on their way to glory in
Barcelona as Colin Stein
shoots them into a twenty-
fourth minute lead against
Moscow Dynamo in the
1972 European Cup-
Winners' Cup final.

TOM FORSYTH   He hated the nickname of 'Jaws' which he earned in Scottish football, and Tom was much more than a fearsome tackler. He invariably won the ball and set up attacks for Rangers. He signed for £40,000 from Motherwell in 1972 and won all the domestic honours, plus twenty-two caps for Scotland, before retiring through injury in 1982.

JOCK WALLACE   A typical shot of 'The Big Man' as he exhorts his troops to greater efforts. His feat of winning the 'treble' of Premier League, Scottish Cup and League Cup twice will be hard to equal.

7
Jock and John

If Jock Wallace had to do anything to ensure championship success again for Rangers, it was to instil consistency into a side which found that quality dreadfully hard to find. His task was quickly spelt out to him as the 1972–73 season began with the traditional League Cup section ties. Clydebank, St Mirren and Ayr United stood in the way of Rangers and the second round and although his players made it safely in the end, they caused the new boss a few headaches on the way. It was as hard for him to understand as it was for the Rangers supporters as the Light Blues won 4–0 against St Mirren in Paisley, then seven days later crashed 4–1 to the same opponents at Ibrox!

Wallace knew that kind of topsy-turvy form would be disastrous in the League and his worst fears were confirmed on the opening day of the championship when, despite taking an early lead through Willie Johnston, Rangers lost 2–1 to Ayr United at Somerset Park. Three of the first five fixtures in the League were lost, including a 3–1 reverse at the hands of Celtic, which made the title chase an uphill struggle from the start.

Second Division Stenhousemuir were conquered over two legs in the second round of the League Cup, despite an embarrassing home defeat, and problems also piled up on Wallace off the field. Alfie Conn handed in a transfer request, Willie Johnston was banned for nine weeks for yet another sending-off and striker Colin Stein was unhappy at Ibrox.

Wallace must have wondered what he had taken on, but he grabbed the proverbial bull by the horns, first of all selling Stein to Coventry City. The deal was worth £140,000 to Rangers as they collected a cheque for £90,000 along with former Ayr United winger Quinton 'Cutty' Young. Veteran striker Joe Mason was snapped up from Morton and talented defender Tom Forsyth signed for £40,000 from Motherwell. The latter player, in particular, would prove to be a superb buy.

Form in the League improved dramatically, but the League Cup campaign ended at the semi-final stage. Rangers badly missed injured skipper John Greig and John Brownlie's seventieth-minute goal deservedly took Hibs into the final which they won. Their last match of 1972 saw Rangers reverse the score against Ayr United, happy-again Alfie Conn and Derek Parlane grabbing the goals in the 2–1 win, which left them third in the championship table.

Wallace had shaken the dressing-room up and was charting a far more healthier course to glory. Willie Johnston's protracted move to West Bromwich Albion had finally gone through, with Cutty Young having established himself in the number eleven jersey. He scored the only goal of the New Year's Day game against Partick Thistle at Firhill and then played his part in a morale-boosting 2–1 win over Celtic at Ibrox. Derek Parlane gave Rangers a first-half lead and although an own goal from Dave Smith levelled affairs, Alfie Conn dramatically headed home a Young cross in the final minute.

The Ibrox men were buoyant as they faced up to mighty Ajax of Amsterdam over two legs in January. The Super Cup was a new competition, created partly by the efforts of Willie Waddell, and it was some compensation for Rangers' European ban, reduced to the one season.

Led by the genius of Johann Cruyff, supplemented by superstars like Ruud Krol, Arie Haan and Johnny Rep, Ajax were the World Club Champions. A crowd of 58,000 witnessed the first leg at Ibrox and saw the Dutch masters display their full array of skills. Rangers competed admirably and when Alex MacDonald equalized Johnny Rep's superb opener, they looked as though they could match Ajax. It proved false optimism and further goals from the magnificent Cruyff and then Arie Haan earned Ajax a 3–1 win and a huge ovation from the Rangers supporters. They knew they had seen a special footballing side in action and many of them made the trip to Holland for the second instalment.

Again, Rangers were anything but disgraced as this time they lost 3–2. Alex MacDonald actually gave them the lead, Haan equalized, Young put Rangers in front once more before Gerry Muhren and Cruyff found a way past Peter McCloy. It had been an enjoyable interlude for the players, but it was soon back to the real business of League and Scottish Cup.

By the end of February, Rangers were top of the championship table and had manoeuvred their way past Dundee United and Hibernian in the first rounds of the Scottish Cup.

The consistency Jock Wallace had demanded had been produced by his players and while Celtic were still favourites for the title, with games in hand and a better goal difference, Rangers fancied themselves strongly to win the Centenary Scottish Cup.

Airdrie were beaten 2–0 in the quarter-finals, then Derek Parlane scored both goals in the semi-final at Hampden as 51,815 fans watched Ayr United overcome. When an Alfie Conn goal a minute from time earned Rangers a 2–2 draw at Pittodrie on 21 April, it was the first point they had lost since a goalless affair against Aberdeen at Ibrox in mid-December. In between times, Rangers had won sixteen successive League games, but that superb form still wasn't enough to wrest the title from Celtic, who took it by a point in the final analysis. It made the Ibrox men all the more determined to beat their 'Old Firm' rivals in the Scottish Cup final on 5 May – but before then, there were more comings

HUNDRED YEARS ON   The Rangers players line up before the start of the 1973 Centenary match against Arsenal.

SUPER NIGHT   The 1973 Super Cup match between Rangers and Ajax at Ibrox is kicked off by Light Blues legend Andy Cunningham. Johann Cruyff, Guy Thys, Jock Shaw and John Greig look on approvingly.

Above DEREK PARLANE Signed from Queen's Park in 1970, Derek was a talented striker who just missed out on selection for the Cup-Winners' Cup team, although he scored in the semi-final. He spent ten successful years at Ibrox, winning two League Championship, three Scottish Cup and two League Cup winners medals in addition to twelve caps for Scotland before signing for Leeds United in 1980 for £160,000.

Left SANDY JARDINE A total of 773 games and 33 goals for Rangers can't even begin to sum up Sandy's contribution to the Ibrox cause. He made his début in the wake of the disastrous 1967 Scottish Cup defeat and matured into one of the world's great right-backs but could also play in midfield. Sandy won three League Championship, five Scottish Cup and four League Cup winners medals, as well as playing in the 1972 Cup-Winners' Cup triumph, before signing for Hearts in 1982.

and goings orchestrated by Jock Wallace.

Goalkeeper Stewart Kennedy was snapped up from Stenhousemuir for £10,000 to keep Peter McCloy on his toes, winger Doug Houston bought from Dundee United for £45,000 and strikers Johnny Hamilton and Ally Scott signed on free transfers from Hibs and Queen's Park respectively. A sad farewell was made to centre-half Ronnie McKinnon. So often Rangers' best player in vital matches, he never fully recovered from the broken leg that kept him out of the European Cup-Winners' Cup final. He was given a free transfer and left after 482 games' sterling service to Rangers, the highlight being when he captained them to League Cup success against Celtic in 1970.

The Light Blues were now ready for another 'Old Firm' cup final and this was the team who lined up at Hampden in front of 122,714 fans: Peter McCloy, Sandy Jardine, Willie Mathieson, John Greig, Derek Johnstone, Alex Mac-Donald, Tommy McLean, Tom Forsyth, Derek Parlane, Alfie Conn, Quinton Young.

It was a classic contest, totally fitting in the hundredth year of Scotland's oldest competition. Celtic enjoyed early pressure and Kenny Dalglish gave them a twenty-fourth-minute lead. Ten minutes later, the Rangers fans were cheering once more when a super move involving Mathieson and MacDonald ended with Derek Parlane heading the equalizer past Ally Hunter.

The second half couldn't have started better for Rangers. Only twenty seconds had elapsed when Young and Parlane combined to leave Alfie Conn with a clear sight of goal and the ball whizzed past Hunter into the net. It was action-packed, dramatic stuff and Rangers' momentum was stilled in the fifty-fourth minute when George Connelly beat Peter McCloy from the penalty-spot after John Greig had handled. The crowd were loving every minute – well, almost, depending upon which end they stood at!

To the jubilation of those wearing red, white and blue, it was Rangers who penned the final chapter with an extraordinary winning goal, never to be forgotten in the history of the Scottish Cup. Tommy McLean chipped in a free-kick from the right for Derek Johnstone to tower majestically and get in a header. The ball struck a post, rolled slowly along the line and with time seemingly suspended, Tom Forsyth appeared to make the decisive contact. Skipper John Greig wept tears of joy at the end before climbing the Hampden steps to collect the Scottish Cup. It was the twentieth time Rangers had won the trophy – the first time since Kai Johansen's dramatic winner in 1966.

Jock Wallace's first season in charge had to be termed a success, although no one, least of all the manager himself, would be happy until Rangers were champions again.

The summer of 1973 saw changes at boardroom level with John Lawrence relinquishing the reins as chairman and becoming the club's first honorary president. Matt Taylor was the new incumbent of the chair.

After the initial encouragement of his first term at the helm, 1973–74 was a massive disappointment to Jock Wallace and everyone at Ibrox. In a closely fought League Cup section, Celtic were edged into second place on goal difference, although both clubs progressed to the second round at any rate. A 3–1 win at Parkhead in the section gave grounds for optimism that Rangers could halt Celtic's bid for a ninth successive championship win. That hope was sent crashing around the ears of the Ibrox men and Wallace as they contrived a dreadful start to their League campaign from which it was impossible to recover. They failed to score in their opening four League matches, picking up just one point in the process and Celtic were soon racing clear at the top of the table while Rangers struggled to get away from the also-rans. It was terribly disheartening, but at least there were other distractions for the players and fans in the shape of the League Cup and European Cup-Winners' Cup.

Welcomed back to the European stage after the excellent behaviour of the supporters who travelled to Amsterdam for the Super Cup match the previous season, Rangers first assignment was a trip to Turkey. The unknowns of Ankaragucu posed few problems and goals each side of half-time from Alfie Conn and Tommy McLean gave the Light Blues a 2–0 win in the first leg to make the Ibrox match a formality. Just 30,000 watched the second leg when a double from John Greig and goals from 'wonder boy' Alex O'Hara and Derek Johnstone completed a 6–0 aggregate win with two Turks being sent-off along the way.

There was no such easy ride in the second round, with Borussia Moenchengladbach having improved greatly from the side humiliated 11–0 over two matches by Rangers thirteen years before. This was now a team that commanded the respect of European football and the Germans showed why in front of 33,000 fans in the imposing Boekelburg Stadium. Jupp Heynckes was too hot a forward for Rangers to handle, scoring twice and seeing a penalty-kick saved by Peter McCloy. Rupp also found the net to leave Jock Wallace's men with a three-goal deficit to make up in Glasgow.

Typically of Wallace, he refused to accept the game was a lost cause and as a result the 40,000 who loyally turned up for the tie were rewarded with a wonderful ninety minutes. Alfie Conn gave Rangers hope with a tenth-minute goal only for Jensen to re-establish Borussia's three-goal lead eighteen minutes later. The home side piled forward in numbers and Colin Jackson and Alex MacDonald found a way past keeper Kleff to put Rangers 3–1 up on the night and send the fans into raptures. The dream was abruptly crushed, though, twenty minutes from the end when the brilliant Danish winger, Jensen, slotted in his second, despite heroics from Peter McCloy, to clinch the tie for the Germans 5–3.

Wallace could have no complaints about the commitment of his players and it was that quality which pushed them on to the semi-finals of the League Cup with aggregate wins over Dumbarton and Hibs. The will-to-win deserted them, though, as a hat-trick from Harry Hood gave Celtic a decidedly easy 3–1 win and a place in the Hampden final.

By the turn of the year, the gap between Rangers and Celtic in the championship was six points and a twenty-seventh minute goal by Bobby Lennox at Parkhead on 5 January all but clinched the title for Jock Stein's side.

Derek Parlane was one player whose form was unaffected by the general inconsistency and he went on to finish top scorer with twenty-two goals. That included an amazing four-goal haul in a 4–2 win over Hearts at Tynecastle on 19 January and when Parlane grabbed a hat-trick in the following week's 8–0 destruction of Queen's Park in the opening round of the Scottish Cup, there was hope that his goals could help Rangers win the only trophy left to them. In common with the rest of the season, that would all turn sour too.

The next tie, against Dundee at Ibrox, was switched to a Sunday – the first time this had happened – and a bumper gate of 64,672 saw Rangers flop miserably, Jocky Scott and John Duncan (two) scoring the goals which took the Dens men comfortably through.

Rangers then faced a battle just to ensure qualification for Europe – and despite winning their last four League games, they were squeezed out by Hibs who finished a point above them in second place in the League. It was hardly the kind of progress report to make happy reading for Jock Wallace and when the following season began with no new signings at Ibrox, there were murmurings of discontent from many supporters.

Rangers prepared for a crucial season with a tour of Sweden and the first-team squad lost a member when Alfie Conn was sold to Spurs for £140,000. Elimination from the League Cup at the qualifying stage, beaten home and away by Hibs, brought further misery upon the Light Blues and it was impossible to forecast a successful championship campaign.

Once the League fixtures got underway, though, Rangers appeared to be a transformed side. When they recorded their first win at Parkhead in six years, in their third game of the championship, the faith of their supporters was restored all of a sudden. Wallace's men displayed a resilience and skill against Celtic, coming back from Kenny Dalglish's thirty-first-minute opener to win 2–1 with Ian McDougall and Colin Jackson scoring the vital goals. Six days later, right-winger Bobby McKean was signed from St Mirren for £40,000 and Rangers looked a good bet for the title!

Stewart Kennedy established himself in goal and turned in some superb performances, Sandy Jardine and Colin Jackson were outstanding at the back, McKean added an injection of pace and zest up front where Derek Parlane continued to score freely – including five in a 6–1 win at Dunfermline! Could Rangers now grasp the consistency they had lacked for so long?

By the turn of the year, just two matches had been lost, yet Celtic were still two points out in front at the top of the table – the 'Old Firm' meeting at Ibrox on 4 January was to prove crucial.

Rangers got the perfect start in front of the 70,000 crowd when Derek Johnstone headed home a Tommy McLean cross after just six minutes. Celtic stormed back and it was then that the decision to give Captain Marvel, John Greig, a man-marking job on the brilliant Kenny Dalglish paid off. Greig dogged the Celtic star's every step and when the half-time whistle arrived, the Parkhead men had shot their bolt. Five minutes after the break, McLean converted an Alex MacDonald pass to make it 2–0 then set-up another for Derek Parlane to leave Rangers comfortable winners.

There was no stopping Rangers after that and the only disappointment came in the shape of a third-round Scottish Cup defeat at the hands of Aberdeen,

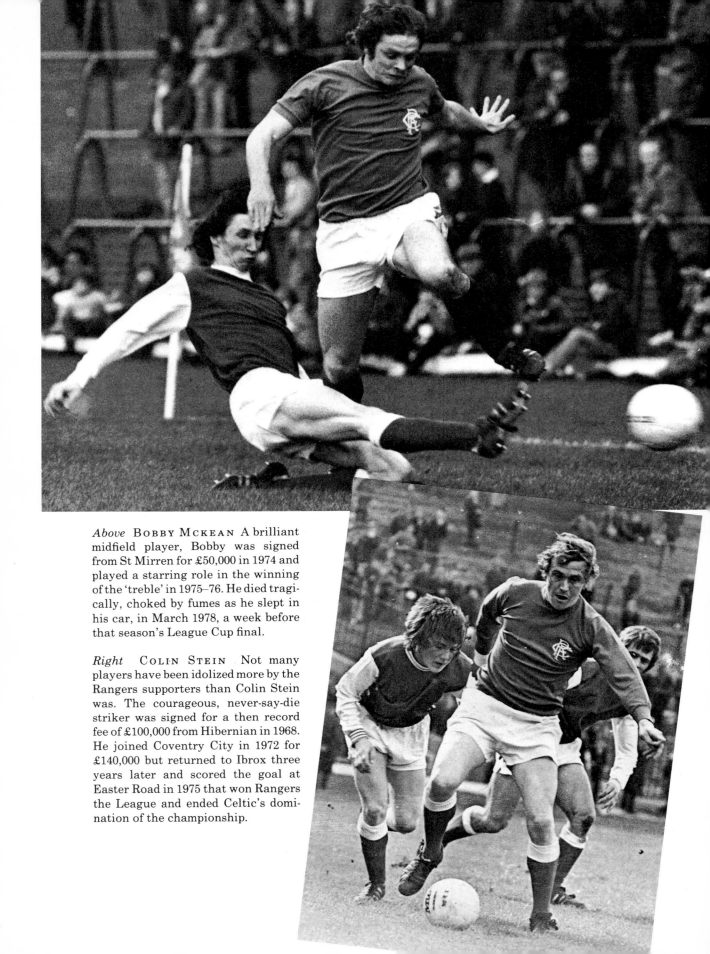

Above BOBBY MCKEAN A brilliant midfield player, Bobby was signed from St Mirren for £50,000 in 1974 and played a starring role in the winning of the 'treble' in 1975–76. He died tragically, choked by fumes as he slept in his car, in March 1978, a week before that season's League Cup final.

Right COLIN STEIN Not many players have been idolized more by the Rangers supporters than Colin Stein was. The courageous, never-say-die striker was signed for a then record fee of £100,000 from Hibernian in 1968. He joined Coventry City in 1972 for £140,000 but returned to Ibrox three years later and scored the goal at Easter Road in 1975 that won Rangers the League and ended Celtic's domination of the championship.

who won 2–1 in an Ibrox replay. The supporters would willingly forgive that if the League Championship was captured for the first time since 1964 and with Rangers four points clear of Celtic with eight games left, Jock Wallace took out his own insurance premium on the title. Colin Stein, the supporters' prodigal son, returned to Ibrox from Coventry City on 5 March for £80,000, just two and a half years after his original move to Highfield Road.

Two weeks after Stein's return, Rangers travelled to Easter Road knowing that a point against Hibernian, by this time second in the table, would clinch their thirty-fifth League triumph. They went into the match without the injured John Greig and it seemed unthinkable that a day of joy could pass without the involvement of the player who had carried the team through so many lean seasons.

The travelling fans made up a large part of the 38,585 crowd and they saw things start poorly for Rangers. With nineteen minutes on the clock, Eric Schaedler sent over an accurate cross and the ball was smacked under Stewart Kennedy by the head of Ally McLeod. Hibs were clearly intent on making their slim championship hopes last as long as possible, but Rangers fought back furiously only for Scotland's Player of the Year, Sandy Jardine, to miss a penalty-kick. But glory was to belong to Rangers and in the sixty-first minute came a moment the Rangers fans who witnessed it will never forget. Bobby McKean floated over a cross from the right and there rose Colin Stein to meet the ball with his head. It flew past the despairing Jim McArthur to give Stein his first goal since returning. It was the goal that won the championship.

Emotions ran high among the Rangers fans and the best moment of all came when John Greig replaced Sandy Jardine for the last couple of minutes to take a deserved share of the magic moment. The line-up on that glorious day at Easter Road, when Celtic's domination of the championship was ended, was: Stewart Kennedy, Sandy Jardine (John Greig), Colin Jackson, Tom Forsyth, Alex Miller, Bobby McKean, Alex MacDonald, Tommy McLean, Derek Parlane (Quinton Young), Derek Johnstone, Colin Stein. It was also historic, in as much as Rangers had won the last championship before the reconstruction of the Leagues that saw the introduction of the Premier Division.

Over 63,000 fans turned up for a gala day at Ibrox in the last match of the season and although opponents Airdrie spoiled the party a little by winning 1–0, nothing could diminish the joy of the Rangers fans.

Rangers approached the start of the new-look Scottish domestic programme with justified confidence that their heroes could dominate the scene – how right they were to be, initially at any rate.

Jock Wallace started 1975–76 with just one new signing, midfielder Kenny Watson who was signed from Montrose for £30,000 but who went into the reserves for experience. Peter McCloy returned in goal, following a shattering blow to Kennedy's morale when he was in the Scotland team which lost 5–1 to England at Wembley at the end of the previous season. That apart, it was the championship-winning side which went into the new term and they cruised through their League Cup section unbeaten in their six ties.

The League campaign couldn't have got off to a better start, 69,000 at Ibrox watching Celtic being beaten 2–1 with goals from Derek Johnstone and Quinton Young, despite the dismissal of Alex MacDonald.

There was sadness in the boardroom when chairman Matt Taylor died early in September. Rae Simpson took over with Willie Waddell becoming the new Vice-Chairman.

The day after his appointment, Rangers entered the European Cup for the first time in eleven seasons, effectively sealing their first-round tie with a 4–1 win over Bohemians Dublin at Ibrox. Sadly, the second round saw Rangers thoroughly outclassed by the brilliant French champions St Etienne, who showed the Ibrox supporters the gulf which still stood between the Scottish champions and top Continental football.

However, domestically the Light Blues marched on and at Hampden on 25 October they took on Celtic in the League Cup final. John Greig lifted the trophy for the first time to complete his set of medals, Alex MacDonald scoring the only goal of a dour match in the sixty-seventh minute.

The Parkhead men led the Premier League by three points by the end of 1975, but when the 'Old Firm' met at Ibrox on New Year's Day, Rangers were on a run of success not to be interrupted. Derek Johnstone scored the only goal of the match and Rangers powered towards the championship, remaining unbeaten right to the end of the season. The flag was clinched at Tannadice on 24 April when top scorer Johnstone found the net after just twenty-two seconds for the only goal of the game against Dundee United.

It left Jock Wallace and his team just ninety minutes away from an historic 'treble' – Hearts at Hampden in the Scottish Cup final on 1 May. The Rangers supporters were in full voice and nothing was going to prevent it being a day of carnival joy for them and their idols. The domestic 'treble' had last been achieved by Rangers in 1963–64, with Celtic repeating the feat in 1966–67. Poor Hearts were merely a sideshow when the big day came.

The amazing Derek Johnstone set the ball rolling again, heading a Tommy McLean free-kick past Jim Cruickshank after just forty-two seconds! From that moment on, it was party time. Alex MacDonald made it 2–0 on the stroke of half-time, Johnstone scored again nine minutes from time and despite Graham Shaw grabbing a consolation goal for Hearts, it was an amazing achievement for Rangers and a proud day for Jock Wallace.

Skipper John Greig was named as Scotland's Player of the Year, a fitting tribute to the great contribution he made to Rangers Football Club during the season.

The overwhelming success meant that anything less in the following season would be hailed as disappointment by fans now gorged on triumph. In the event, 1976–77 was something of a disaster, which was as sharp in contrast to the previous term as you could imagine.

Rangers had a smooth ride through their League Cup section and were unbeaten, but then they were eliminated from the European Cup by FC Zurich in the first round and their season began to turn very sour.

Four games were needed to overcome First Division Clydebank in the League Cup quarter-final, but the semi-final was nowhere near so drawn out – Aberdeen hammered the Light Blues 5–1 at Hampden with Jocky Scott grabbing a hat-trick.

Celtic were four points clear in the Premier League race by early January and when an own goal from Colin Jackson gave the Parkhead men victory in the 'Old Firm' encounter later in the month, things looked bleak. Celtic eventually finished nine points clear of Rangers, leaving the 'Old Firm' Scottish Cup final as the Ibrox men's last chance of glory.

In a match fraught with tension on both sides, the only goal arrived in the twentieth minute and caused fury in the Rangers camp when Derek Johnstone was judged to have handled a shot from Jo Edvaldsson. The penalty award stood and Andy Lynch drove the ball past Stewart Kennedy from the spot to complete a season of abject misery for Rangers.

The pendulum of success had swung back towards Celtic Park and Jock Wallace knew he had to freshen up his side to restore their pride in 1977–78. That freshness duly arrived with the signings of Davie Cooper, Bobby Russell and Gordon Smith.

Winger Cooper had dazzled everyone with his displays in the First Division for Clydebank and also in that marathon League Cup tie against Rangers. Jock Wallace had no hesitation in signing him up for £100,000 while midfielder Russell was plucked from junior football with Shettleston. His silky skills would prove vital and memorable in the season to come and the contribution of Smith, bought for £65,000 from Kilmarnock, was crucial too.

And yet things started off badly, with irate supporters chanting for Jock Wallace's resignation after the first two Premier League matches of the season had been lost. At that stage, the possibility of Rangers achieving another 'treble' was laughable – *but that's exactly what a rejuvenated side went on to accomplish*. From beating Celtic 3–2 at Ibrox in the first 'Old Firm' clash of the season, with Gordon Smith scoring twice, Rangers never looked back. With the new signings all making their presence felt, the rest of the players got a lift and the team began to turn on some terrific football, including a 6–1 thrashing of Aberdeen in the League Cup.

Some of the playing-staff were ultimately casualties – Alex O'Hara was sold to Partick Thistle, while the demise of strikers Colin Stein and Martin Henderson began with loan periods to Kilmarnock and Hibernian respectively. By the time Celtic were beaten 3–1 at Ibrox on 7 January, the Premier League title was virtually a foregone conclusion and Rangers also cruised into the final of the League Cup.

Two days before that Hampden date against Celtic, tragedy struck when Bobby McKean was found dead in his car outside his house. It was a shattering blow for everyone at Ibrox, but the players summoned up all their pride and passion to complete the first leg of the 'treble'. In a fitting tribute to their late friend and team-mate, they defeated Celtic 2–1 after extra-time with Davie Cooper and Gordon Smith the men on target.

Aberdeen produced an admirable charge for the championship, which included a stunning 3–0 win at Ibrox, but the last day of the League season saw Rangers at home to Motherwell knowing exactly what they had to do to clinch

JOHN GREIG
TESTIMONIAL
1978

GORDON SMITH   An intelligent midfield player, Gordon Smith was signed from Kilmarnock for £65,000 in 1977 and proved a real bargain. His creative skills were allied to an eye for goal himself and he played a big part in the team winning the 'treble' in his first season. He was sold to Brighton for £400,000 in 1980 and had an unsuccessful return to Ibrox on loan in December 1982 when he played in the League Cup final which Celtic won 2–1.

Opposite above   CELEBRATION TIME   The first leg of the historic 'treble' in 1975–6 is completed as Alex MacDonald celebrates scoring the only goal of the League Cup final against Celtic with Danny McGrain looking on.

Opposite below   THANK YOU   That is John Greig's simple message to the massed ranks of Rangers fans who turned up for his testimonial match in 1978 against a Scotland XI. It was a fitting tribute to perhaps the club's greatest ever captain. Greig played 857 first-team games for Rangers. He won five League Championships, six Scottish Cup and three League Cup winners medals. He captained the club to their greatest ever triumph in Barcelona in 1972. He won forty-four caps for Scotland. A superb footballer, an inspirational leader and a loyal servant, Greig was twenty-three years at Ibrox as player and manager and his name will always be up at the top when great Rangers are being discussed.

the title. By the end of the afternoon, the loudspeakers at the stadium were blasting out the sound of 'Congratulations'. Colin Jackson and Gordon Smith scored the goals in a 2–0 win and Rangers were champions of Scotland for the thirty-seventh time.

It was a season for achievements and the following week at Hampden, Jock Wallace became the first Rangers manager to win two 'trebles' when Aberdeen were beaten 2–1 in the Scottish Cup final.

The slight figure of Bobby Russell was the outstanding player on a glorious afternoon. He controlled the play like a general on a battlefield manoeuvring his troops. Alex MacDonald gave Rangers a half-time lead before Scotland's 'Player of the Year', Derek Johnstone, netted his thirty-eighth goal of the season. Steve Ritchie pulled a late goal back for the Dons, but it was John Greig who again climbed the Hampden steps to collect the trophy – it was his third 'treble' in a glittering playing career. Little could he have imagined the fateful twist his career was about to take.

On 23 May 1978, Jock Wallace stunned Scottish football when he resigned as manager of Rangers. To this day, he has never revealed the reason behind his decision, but it's fair to assume he didn't see eye-to-eye with the board over what he was worth after such a successful season. Just twenty-four hours later, John Greig was catapulted from the dressing-room to the manager's office. His fantastic playing career was over, now he was the boss of the club he loved.

It was a sensational change, without a doubt, and while Wallace was lured south to take charge of Leicester City, Greig had to keep Rangers at the top of the tree in Scotland. His first task was to appoint a successor to himself as club captain and, to many people's surprise, the honour went to Derek Johnstone. The only addition he made to the playing-staff was up front where Billy Urquhart was signed from Highland League kings Inverness Caley.

One of Greig's main aims was to push Rangers back to the forefront of European football, from which they had slipped in recent seasons, latterly being knocked out of the European Cup-Winners' Cup in the first round by Twente Enschede in Wallace's final season in charge. A first-round draw against mighty Juventus couldn't have been tougher for Greig, but it was in the European Cup where his team would shine brightest in a dramatic first season as manager.

In front of 62,000 fans in the Stadio Communale, the Light Blues followed Greig's defensive tactics to the letter and after ninety minutes of exhausting effort had restricted Juventus to a 1–0 lead to take to Glasgow.

The Italians, with nine World Cup stars in their line-up, still fancied their chances for the second leg but 44,000 fans in the new-look Ibrox, taking shape quickly, were treated to a night of joy. Alex MacDonald levelled the aggregate scores with a seventeenth-minute goal and from that moment on, Juventus were a worried side who ended up out-classed, Gordon Smith grabbing the decisive second goal in the second half.

The second round promised nothing easier than the first, with Dutch masters PSV Eindhoven coming to Ibrox for the first leg. This time, there was only frustration for the capacity crowd as Rangers dominated but couldn't find the route to goal and the game finished goalless.

It looked to be a hopeless task as Rangers flew out to Holland a fortnight later with the knowledge that PSV had never been beaten on their own ground in a European tie. When Harry Lubse gave the Dutch side the lead in the very first minute, Rangers' European dream looked to be down and out. That, though, was just the start of one of the most memorable matches in Rangers' history. Alex MacDonald levelled the scores in the fifty-seventh minute and even when Deykers put PSV in front once more three minutes later, the poise, skill and determination displayed by the Scottish champions never wavered. Derek Johnstone made it 2–2 in the sixty-sixth minute and in a fantastic finale, Bobby Russell coolly shot Rangers into the quarter-finals of the European Cup three minutes from the end.

There was now total belief within the Rangers camp that they could go on to win the European Cup, even when they were drawn against the tournament favourites, Cologne, in the quarter-finals.

Thanks to a superb performance by Peter McCloy, they came back from the first leg in West Germany having lost just 1–0 to a headed goal from the deadly Dieter Muller. It gave Rangers every chance for the return in Glasgow, but sadly that turned out to be a night of dreadful frustration as the inexperience of Billy Urquhart cost them dearly.

The striker had two excellent chances to find a way past Cologne keeper Toni Schumacher, but his nerve failed him at the crucial moments. Dieter Muller struck two minutes into the second half and when Tommy McLean scored for Rangers three minutes from the end, it was no more than an empty gesture. Greig and Rangers had to return to earth and concentrate on the task of defending their three domestic honours.

Well placed in the Premier League, Rangers took on Aberdeen in the final of the League Cup at Hampden ten days after their European Cup exit. The Ibrox men took command from the start, but found Bobby Clark and Willie Miller in particular providing stiff resistance at the back for the Dons. The Pittodrie side stunned the huge Rangers support in the 54,000 crowd when Duncan Davidson fired them into the lead in the fifty-ninth minute. The goal, though, seemed to do more for Rangers and they equalized in the seventy-seventh minute with yet another vital goal from that most tenacious of midfield players, Alex MacDonald. Aberdeen appeared to crumble and Doug Rougvie was shown the red card following an incident with Derek Johnstone. With extra-time looming large, Colin Jackson scored a dramatic winning goal in the dying seconds to give John Greig his first major trophy as manager and Derek Johnstone his first as skipper.

The Premier Division race had turned into an exciting battle with Rangers, Celtic and Dundee United all involved. When United were beaten 2–1 at Tannadice and Celtic 1–0 at Ibrox in the run-in, it looked as if the flag would stay at Ibrox. Rangers had also reached the Scottish Cup final and after two matches had ended goalless against Hibs, that had to be left in the melting pot while the Light Blues travelled to Parkhead knowing a point would secure the

GLORY GOAL Alex Mac-
Donald rises to beat Juventus
defender Marco Tardelli to the
ball and head Rangers' first goal
against the Italian giants in the
European Cup-tie at Ibrox in
1978. The Light Blues won 2–1 on
aggregate.

IN COMMAND Peter McCloy
in action against Danny McGrain
of Celtic, two great 'Old Firm' servants together. McCloy fought off
several challengers for the goalkeeper's jersey at Ibrox and
moved on to the coaching staff
before leaving Ibrox in August
1988.

SUPER IBROX   The magnificent Ibrox Stadium, renewed and rebuilt at a cost of £12 million and now one of the finest playing arenas in the world.

DEADLY ALLY   The second Rangers goal in their 2–0 win over Celtic at Ibrox on New Year's Day, 1987. Ally McCoist pounces on a mistake by goalkeeper Pat Bonner to smash his shot into the net.

championship. Celtic knew a victory for them would mean the crown going to the other end of Glasgow and it all added up to a pulsating ninety minutes.

Bobby Russell gave Rangers the perfect start with a ninth-minute goal and that's how the scoreline stood until the sixty-sixth minute when Roy Aitken equalized for Celtic. By that stage, Celtic were down to ten men after the dismissal of Johnny Doyle, but they went 2–1 up through George McCluskey. Alex MacDonald equalized for Rangers fourteen minutes from time and a 2–2 scoreline would have given them the title. But a tragic own goal from Colin Jackson was embellished by a last-minute strike from Murdo MacLeod and Celtic had wrenched the championship away.

Consolation was gained seven days later when the second replay of the Scottish Cup final ended in a 3–2 win after extra-time, Derek Johnstone scoring twice and an own goal from Arthur Duncan providing the winner. Despite the disappointment of the Premier League loss, it had to be considered a successful first season as boss by Greig – but, by stark contrast, 1979–80 was a nightmare.

This time, the European Cup-Winners' Cup campaign provided the *only* moments worth savouring as Rangers finished a dreadful fifth in the Premier League, eleven points behind champions Aberdeen and ten behind Celtic. Greig couldn't get his men to repeat their superbly disciplined and skilful European form in the domestic matches.

In the European Cup-Winners' Cup there was nothing but praise for Rangers as they defeated Lillestrom and Fortuna Dusseldorf to set-up a meeting with Spanish aces Valencia. This was the team of Mario Kempes and Rainer Bonhof and a fantastic performance from Peter McCloy in the first leg in Spain, which included a penalty save from Bonhof, earned a 1–1 draw. It left Rangers with a seemingly golden opportunity of another glory night at Ibrox, but Kempes blasted that to pieces with two superb goals in a 3–1 win for Valencia.

With the League Cup having been relinquished at the third-round stage, Aberdeen winning 5–1 on aggregate to avenge their defeat in the previous season's final, it was only the Scottish Cup which could save Rangers season.

There was only one new signing in the side for the final against Celtic, defender Gregor Stevens who had been signed from Leicester City for £150,000. Record buy Ian Redford, finally snapped up from Dundee for £210,000, was cup-tied by the time he arrived at Ibrox and a lot rested on the shoulders of young John MacDonald up front. The talented, tricky Drumchapel kid had answered the need for a new striker with John Greig having cleared the decks with the sale of Derek Parlane to Leeds United for £160,000. MacDonald scored four times on the way to the final, but he could do little for Rangers on a day of shame for Scottish football.

A freakish goal by George McCluskey in extra-time gave Celtic the trophy by a 1–0 verdict after a match which was a credit to both clubs. Sadly, the supporters took it upon themselves to sully the sunny day with a pitch invasion and dreadful scenes of fighting which required mounted police on the Hampden turf. It was the incident which caused the introduction of the Criminal Justice (Scotland) Act which has proved so successful in ensuring such scenes are not repeated.

John Greig's priority, though, was to rebuild his ageing side and he quickly moved into the transfer market to bring striker Colin McAdam from Partick Thistle for £160,000 and midfielder Jim Bett from Lokeren for £180,000 to Ibrox. Moving out for a record fee of £400,000 was Gordon Smith, finding a new challenge with Brighton. The changes continued at the start of the new season with Alex MacDonald moving to Hearts for £30,000 and former star Willie Johnston returning from Vancouver Whitecaps for £40,000.

The 1980–81 Premier League campaign started brightly, with Celtic being defeated home and away, as Rangers remained unbeaten in their first fifteen matches with new striker McAdam grabbing ten goals during that run. Greig's men were rather unlucky to lose 3–2 on aggregate to Aberdeen in the second round of a controversial League Cup tie in which the Dons were awarded two penalty-kicks. The elimination from the Anglo-Scottish Cup – a poor substitute for European football – was downright embarrassing as English Third Division side Chesterfield chalked up a 4–1 aggregate win. It signalled a dramatic slump for Rangers and the 1–0 defeat at the hands of Morton at Ibrox was the beginning of the end of their championship hopes.

Again the Scottish Cup provided the only escape route from disaster and this time Rangers made it through the tunnel. With new goalkeeper Jim Stewart in the ranks, a £115,000 signing from Middlesbrough, Rangers survived a fourth-round hiccup against St Johnstone to reach the Scottish Cup final.

After a goalless draw in which Ian Redford had a last-minute penalty-kick saved by Hamish McAlpine, Rangers turned on one of their greatest displays under John Greig's management to defeat Dundee United 4–1 in the replay. Davie Cooper and John MacDonald responded to their recall in brilliant style. Cooper opened the scoring, Bobby Russell added a second and MacDonald netted twice to put the game beyond a shattered United side.

It was a morale-boosting end to the season for Greig and his side, and the Rangers manager strengthened his squad for an intended push on the title by signing Northern Ireland international defender John McClelland from Mansfield Town for £90,000. Greig also tried to buy Scotland's most talked-about young player, St Johnstone's Ally McCoist, but the striker headed south to Sunderland for £100,000 more than Rangers had offered. Still, Rangers breezed through their 1981–82 League Cup section unbeaten and that included an 8–1 crushing of Raith Rovers at Ibrox in which Davie Cooper produced the most memorable individual performance seen in the stadium for years.

It should have been the dawning of a bright new era for the club with the space-age stadium completed. Instead, there were only cheap jokes about the expensive stands being built facing the wrong way – towards the pitch.

On the day that the £4 million Copland Road Stand was opened in the first 'Old Firm' Premier League meeting of the season, Celtic won easily 2–0 and by December there were seven points between Rangers and their great rivals.

The League Cup, though, had been carried back to the Ibrox trophy room following an admirable comeback in the final against Dundee United, which culminated in a dramatic and spectacular winning goal from Ian Redford.

In Europe, Rangers blew their European Cup-Winners' Cup hopes with a

3–0 defeat at the hands of Dukla Prague in Czechoslovakia, which gave them no chance of pulling back the deficit at home.

John Greig's attempts to strengthen his squad were fruitless and he had the added blows of a six-month suspension for Gregor Stevens and the sad retirement through injury of marvellous servant Tom Forsyth.

Rangers finished third in the League table, twelve points behind champions Celtic and this time there was to be no reprieve in the Scottish Cup final. After taking the lead thanks to a spectacular diving header from John MacDonald in the Hampden final, Aberdeen equalized through Alex McLeish then demoralized Rangers with three goals in extra-time to take the trophy to Pittodrie.

John Greig recognized that it was time for sweeping changes at Ibrox and his free transfer list included long-serving 'greats' in the shape of Sandy Jardine, Colin Jackson, Tom Forsyth and Tommy McLean, the latter becoming Greig's assistant. Swedish international midfielder Robert Prytz was signed from Malmo for £100,000, while the defence was boosted with the arrival of Dave MacKinnon from Partick Thistle for £30,000 and Craig Paterson for a record £225,000 from Hibernian. It seemed to be having the desired effect when Rangers started the 1982–83 season with an unbeaten twenty-match run which included a romp through their League Cup section, a first-round UEFA Cup win over Borussia Dortmund and an encouraging start to the Premier League campaign.

The run was ended at Parkhead on 30 October when Murdo MacLeod scored three minutes from time to give Celtic a 3–2 win in a smashing 'Old Firm' match at Parkhead. The following midweek, Rangers' season was seen to be visibly coming apart at the seams as they were destroyed 5–0 by Cologne in the second leg of their UEFA Cup second-round tie in West Germany.

Rangers did reach the final of the League Cup, but they were two goals down to Celtic before they ever got going and although Jim Bett pulled one back with a superb free-kick, it wasn't enough to prevent the trophy going to Parkhead for the first time in eight seasons.

The championship was a lost cause come New Year, leaving the Scottish Cup once more as Rangers possible salvation – true to form, they reached their eighth successive final. There they faced Aberdeen, newly crowned European Cup-Winners' Cup victors, and Rangers missed a great chance to win the trophy and end their season on a high note. They looked the better side for a long time, only for goalkeeper Jim Leighton to produce a stunning save from a Jim Bett shot which would surely have been the winner. It was tragedy for Bobby Russell, the best player on the field, when his one mistake of the match in extra-time led to Eric Black heading the only goal of the final and keeping the cup in Aberdeen.

John Greig was left with much to contemplate before the 1983–84 season began and he wasn't helped by Jim Bett's return to Lokeren for a fee of £240,000. At least the manager received a boost when Ally McCoist became a Ranger at last, signing from Sunderland for £185,000 – surely one of the greatest bargains of all time. Another member of the 'Old Guard', Derek Johnstone, was sold to Chelsea for £30,000 and a dramatic season for the club was underway.

SUPER COOPER With a jink and a shimmy, Davie Cooper is free of Celtic trio Peter Grant, Tony Shepherd and Paul McStay during the 1986–87 League Cup final.

IAN DURRANT The precocious young midfield player has established himself as one of Europe's best young stars and a favourite with the Rangers supporters. He is destined to have a glittering career at club and international level.

McCoist and Sandy Clark, the latter signed from West Ham United for £160,000 the previous March, seemed to hit it off up front in pre-season matches but when three of the first four Premier League games were lost, the pressure was very firmly on the team and, in particular, the manager.

A huge demonstration followed the 2–0 home defeat to Aberdeen and despite a brief revival, there were even worse scenes following a 2–1 loss to Motherwell at Ibrox on 22 October. Six days later, John Greig resigned as manager of Rangers, ending a continuous period of employment with the club which stretched over more than twenty years. It was an indescribably sad moment for everyone at Ibrox, yet at the same time somehow inevitable.

In a traumatic fortnight in which Tommy McLean did an admirable job in almost impossible circumstances as caretaker manager, Rangers went out of the European Cup-Winners' Cup on the away goals rule to FC Porto.

After Alex Ferguson of Aberdeen and Dundee United's Jim McLean had rejected Rangers' advances, Jock Wallace returned to Ibrox as manager on 10 November 1983. The club had to pay Motherwell £125,000 to buy out his contract, but the fans thought it was worth it and travelled in numbers to Aberdeen to see the Big Man's first match back in charge. Rangers lost 3–0, their fifth successive League defeat, proving there would be no miracles worked by Wallace, regarded by the success-starved fans as the saviour.

Things did improve gradually. Davie Cooper returned to fitness and form, Greig's final signing Jimmy Nicholl settled in well and Wallace appointed Alex Totten and John Hagart as his right-hand men. Out went Gordon Dalziel, Kenny Lyall and Kenny Black while goalkeeper Nicky Walker and striker Bobby Williamson arrived at Ibrox for a total of £250,000. It was too late for the Premier League title to be chased, but Wallace set his sights firmly on the cup competitions and added another newcomer to the squad in the shape of Stuart Munro from Alloa for £15,000.

Two tremendous performances against Dundee United in the two-legged semi-final took Rangers through to the League Cup final to face Celtic, but the week before that match, Dundee came to Ibrox and eliminated the Light Blues from the Scottish Cup. However, the Rangers fans in the 66,369 crowd at Hampden forgot that as their rejuvenated heroes lifted the League Cup for a record twelfth time. Ally McCoist, who finished the season top scorer with twenty-two domestic goals, grabbed all three in a thrilling 3–2 win over Celtic after extra-time.

That triumph was greatly welcomed but couldn't disguise the fact that the Premier League remained the priority for Wallace, especially as the team finished up fifteen points behind champions Aberdeen in fourth place at the end of the season.

Gregor Stevens and Jim Stewart were handed free transfers while Dundee duo Iain Ferguson and Cammy Fraser were bought for a total fee, set by tribunal, of £365,000. The pair certainly pepped up a Rangers side in which youngster David McPherson was continuing to catch the eye, but a crisis struck in September when John McClelland was sacked as club captain, the job going to Craig Paterson. McClelland, an outstanding player for Rangers since his arrival, was looking for a better financial deal and the club's failure to meet his requirements caused a sad rift. He signed for Watford for £265,000 and Jock Wallace also sold striker Sandy Clark to Hearts for £40,000.

Still, in 1984–85 the team made it to the League Cup final yet again and a superb goal from Iain Ferguson paid off a huge chunk of his transfer fee as it was the only one of the match against Dundee United. Shortly afterwards, though, Rangers went out of the UEFA Cup despite an enthralling second-leg fight-back at Ibrox against the superb Italians of Inter Milan.

Eight points off the championship pace after a 2–1 home defeat at the hands of Celtic on New Year's Day, despite the signing of extrovert Ted McMinn and former star Derek Johnstone, things were still way off the desired track for the club. A free-kick from John Brown enabled Dundee to once again end Rangers' Scottish Cup involvement at Ibrox and the season was effectively killed there and then.

The future of the club looked uncertain, but at least young talent like that of Derek Ferguson and Ian Durrant was breaking into the first team to offer some encouragement to the by now depleted and depressed support.

Wallace snapped up midfielder Dougie Bell from Aberdeen for £125,000 at the start of the 1985–86 season and Rangers began well, winning five of their opening six Premier League matches to lead the table. It was then, though, that the old enemy called inconsistency struck with a vengeance.

A first-round exit in the UEFA Cup at the hands of little-known Spanish side Athletico Osasuna was desperately disappointing, while the League Cup was lost when Hibs won a two-legged semi-final 2–1.

In the League, the inability to find any run of decent results was disastrous although there were one-off occasions when the Fergusons and Durrants shone brightly, particularly the 3–0 defeat of Celtic at Ibrox. That wasn't enough, though, to lift any of the pressure mounting on the broad shoulders of Jock Wallace, and a Scottish Cup exit against Hearts at the first hurdle darkened the storm clouds even more.

On Sunday, 6 April, because of their Scottish Cup departure, Rangers arranged a friendly match against Spurs at Ibrox. They were woefully inept in losing 2–0 to the London club and, unknown to the supporters in the stadium that afternoon, Rangers Football Club were about to be rocked on their very foundations. The sleeping giant of Scottish football was about to be shaken out of its doze and dragged dramatically into a whole new era. . . .

8
Rangers are Born Again

When Graeme Souness walked through the door from the manager's office at Ibrox into a packed press conference on Tuesday, 8 April 1986, it was the most stunning and significant moment in Scottish football for decades. The hard-bitten, seen-it-all-before football journalists gasped. There was a discernible pause before the uniform click of the photographers' cameras was heard. Perhaps the Rangers officials on hand still couldn't quite believe it themselves.

The previous day, Jock Wallace had been invited to resign by the Ibrox board of directors. The shambolic 2–0 defeat at the hands of a Spurs side in second gear being seen as the straw which broke the camel's back. As had always been his way, Jock Wallace accepted the events of his second parting of the ways with Rangers with great dignity. There was no hint of malice; no noises of bitterness against the club. His contribution to the history of the club is there for all to see and will never be forgotten by the supporters, one of whom Jock essentially is. But it was time for Rangers to take a new direction and sadly Jock had to make way for a new regime as radically different from any before as could be imagined.

The installation of Graeme Souness as manager, however, was not a hastily made decision resulting from that weekend. The former Spurs, Middlesbrough and Liverpool superstar, captain of Scotland and capped over fifty times, was head-hunted by David Holmes, the man charged with the task of restoring Rangers to the pinnacle of British football.

The origins of the Ibrox revolution can be traced to November 1985 when, upon the instruction of Lawrence Marlborough, grandson of former Rangers chairman John Lawrence, the building group his grandfather had established took effective control of Rangers. Marlborough had resigned as a director of the club two years before but continued to take a keen interest in the affairs of Rangers from his home in Lake Tahoe near the Nevada desert, where he supervised the American end of the Lawrence Group operation. After meeting Jack Gillespie, vice-chairman at Ibrox, a deal was worked out with Gillespie selling 29,000 of his shares to John Lawrence (Glasgow) Ltd with two other batches of 25,500 shares ultimately being transferred to give Lawrence over 50 per cent of Rangers' issued share capital.

Those were the cold statistics of the takeover but it takes more than a few thousand sold shares to change the course of a great football club – Lawrence Marlborough needed to find a man with the ideas and energy to put Rangers on the course to glory again. That man was David Holmes and his appointment to the board in that November shake-up was the first significant sign of better things to come for the club.

Holmes recalls the time clearly: 'The company rightly thought that to have a third of the shares in Rangers and not have a representative on the board of directors represented a bad investment.

'Lawrence Marlborough asked if I would look into the situation at Ibrox and give him an idea of how I thought the club should go. When I came back to him with my findings, I was asked to join the board.

'I took a good look at Rangers as a business venture and it was clear that it needed not only an injection of capital, but an injection of different ideas.

'While the supporters look to players to provide success at a football club, I soon realized that Rangers could take a lot of pressure off the playing staff by boosting the commercial operation.

'It was my belief that Rangers were lying dormant, just waiting for change and after twenty years with the Lawrence Group, the task I had been set was an exciting new challenge.

'I only took an interest in Rangers when I was asked to do so but as soon as Lawrence Marlborough made the request, and I received the backing of my wife and family, I put all of my energies into the club.'

It didn't take long for Holmes to begin his Ibrox revolution and in February, three directors left the board – ex-chairman Rae Simpson, Jim Robinson and Tom Dawson. Freddie Fletcher, the managing director of Treeby, the office supplies division of John Lawrence, joined the board as sales and marketing director and a new course was starting to be charted. But the fans were barely interested in boardroom activity while Rangers continued to struggle along on the field and that was why David Holmes sought out Graeme Souness.

Holmes recalls the dramatic change in manager: 'When I was promoted to any job, the first thing I did was select a good team around me to help me do the job well.

'With a football club, I had to bring a personality who was known in the broadest scale possible. I wanted a man who would break down the parochial barriers put up by Scottish football.

'I sat down to make a list and Graeme Souness was the first name I put down on it. I didn't go any further – he had all the credentials I was looking for.

'He had been in the game at the highest level on a world stage and would provide Rangers with an identifiable profile on and off the playing field.

'That was the great attraction of having a player–manager and I was sure Graeme would relish the challenge of such a big job in his native country where he had never played before.

'However, before I gave Graeme Souness the job, Jock Wallace had to be told of my intentions and I was delighted that was done in the proper manner.

'I told Jock how I saw Rangers progressing and when he had accepted the decision, I discussed the appointment of Graeme Souness with Lawrence Marlborough. He was only too pleased to agree.'

At the time, Graeme Souness was completing a two-year contract with Sampdoria, one of the less fashionable Italian clubs but one whom he had led to triumph in the Italian Cup following a big money move from Liverpool. How would David Holmes persuade him that his future lay at Ibrox and that the time was right to step into management at such a high level?

Explains Holmes: 'I got a hold of Graeme's phone number and initially spoke to his wife as he was not at home. When I did get him, he was taken aback at first but was obviously interested.

'We agreed to meet in London and then talked more about it when I flew to Milan to see him again. We agreed the deal that day in Italy and I flew back to Edinburgh that night a very happy man.'

David Holmes was by now Chief Executive of the club and the media were following his every move – that he managed to announce the appointment of Graeme Souness with such surprise said much for his ability.

Souness couldn't take up his duties immediately, having to return to Italy to play out his contract with Sampdoria before the £300,000 move to Ibrox became complete. In the meantime, David Holmes had another target to recruit – a right-hand man for his new manager.

Says Holmes: 'One thing Graeme didn't have was experience and knowledge of the Scottish Premier Division and we both agreed upon the man who could bring that to the managerial team.

'Walter Smith was a man we both had the highest regard for and there is no one around with a wider knowledge of the Scottish game. I approached Dundee United for permission to speak to Walter and when I asked him if he wanted to come to Ibrox, he didn't think twice.

'I haven't been disappointed. Graeme and Walter have complemented each other superbly and have become the team I knew they would be – they are great for Rangers.'

Alex Totten and John Hagart were the unfortunate casualties from the coaching staff as the new regime took over, and when Walter Smith watched Rangers lose 2–1 to St Mirren at Love Street on 19 April 1986, he saw the full extent of what faced Graeme Souness and himself. Rangers were actually struggling to finish high enough in the Premier League to qualify for European football the following season.

When Graeme Souness flew from Italy to address the playing-staff for the first time, there was no great speech about his plans for the future. He was terse and to the point – 'get us into the UEFA Cup next season then we'll take it from there.'

A fine goal from the extrovert Ted McMinn earned a crucial point in a 1–1 draw against Aberdeen at Pittodrie in the penultimate League match of the season to leave Rangers needing victory over Motherwell at Ibrox on 3 May

DAVID HOLMES The man given the task of restoring Rangers to the forefront of Scottish football: the Lawrence Group executive pulled off a masterstroke with the recruitment of Graeme Souness as player-manager.

WINNING COMBINATION Walter Smith and Graeme Souness celebrate the championship triumph at Pittodrie, a fitting finale to their first season at the Ibrox helm.

BOOT BOY   Terry Butcher sits proudly in the Ibrox boot room after completing his £725,000 move to Rangers from Ipswich Town on 1 August 1986. He has proved an inspiring captain on and off the field.

CHRIS WOODS   The Rangers goalkeeper in action against George McCluskey of Hibernian. His concentration, reflexes, positioning and burning desire for success persuaded Graeme Souness to pay £600,000 for him from Norwich City.

TEAMING UP   Graeme Souness was a long-time admirer of winger Davie Cooper and instilled a new zest in the Rangers star's play when he took over the reins at Ibrox. Cooper is one of Britain's most naturally talented players and it is one of the game's tragedies that he won just twenty caps for Scotland.

THE GOAL THAT WON THE TITLE   A magical moment for every Rangers fan as Terry Butcher powers a brilliant header into the Aberdeen net at Pittodrie on 2 May 1987. The 1–1 draw clinched the Premier League.

to ensure European qualification. Graeme Souness, now free of his Italian obligations, was in charge for the first time but decided to watch from the Ibrox stand as the following eleven men were entrusted with the vital task: Walker, Burns, Munro, MacKinnon, McPherson, Dawson, Bell, Durrant, McCoist, McMinn, Cooper.

On the day, they were comfortable enough winners over Motherwell, with David McPherson and Ally McCoist scoring the goals in a 2–0 win, which none the less provided the final statistics in the worst season in Rangers' history.

The fans anticipated glory and wanted it even more as on the same day as that win over Motherwell, Celtic had snatched the Premier League title from the grasp of Hearts with a dramatic 5–0 win over St Mirren at Love Street. Friday, 9 May, at least gave the loyal Ibrox fans a moment to cherish from a barren season when the Glasgow Cup was won in front of over 40,000 inside Ibrox. Ally McCoist scored a brilliant hat-trick to beat Celtic, the newly-crowned champions, 3–2 but although it was a highly acceptable success, Graeme Souness knew it could only be a small taste of what he wanted to achieve. Free transfers were handed to Derek Johnstone, Dave MacKinnon, Andy Bruce and Billy Davies as the new boss began to tailor the playing-staff to suit his demands.

Graeme Souness and Walter Smith both had to put Rangers to the back of their minds as much as possible, however, when they joined the Scotland party for the World Cup finals in Mexico. Souness was captain of the Scots side while Smith was manager Alex Ferguson's assistant and, like the professionals they are, they gave Scotland's cause their full concern.

The first major transfer deal had been completed, though, and while they were in Mexico, David Holmes introduced striker Colin West to the media, purchased from Watford for £200,000. But the fun for the newspapers had only started and almost every player in world football, from Peter Shilton to Paulo Roberto Falcao, was linked with Rangers.

The next capture came in July 1986 and was one of the most significant as Chris Woods smashed the record transfer fee for a goalkeeper when he completed a £600,000 move to Ibrox from Norwich City. The English number two international goalkeeper would prove to be an outstanding buy and was the ideal foundation for Souness as he looked to find success by creating a powerful and safe defence.

While Souness would be playing himself, he needed a leader on the field to relieve him of some of the responsibility and the man he wanted as captain was Terry Butcher. With Manchester United and Spurs already in the hunt for the big Ipswich and England centre-half, Rangers were given little chance of capturing Butcher's signature. However, the persuasive powers of Graeme Souness were not to be taken lightly and after a meeting in London, and a trip to Ibrox by the player, Terry Butcher signed for Rangers on 1 August for £725,000. David Holmes described the buy as a 'stroke of genius' on the part of Graeme Souness and he would prove to be correct.

The new man didn't have it all his own way in the transfer market as he was turned down by Dundee United in his bid for Richard Gough, while a work permit problem ruled out Avi Cohen, the Israeli international captain and a former team-mate of Souness at Anfield.

Rangers took the players to West Germany to prepare for the new season and three warm-up matches against minor opposition were augmented by a 2–0 defeat at the hands of Cologne, which showed just how far the team had to go. Cammy Fraser, a midfield man who would play a valuable part in Souness's first season in charge, scored Rangers goal in a 1–1 draw against Spurs in London as the preparations continued.

Terry Butcher's début was made on 5 August when the mighty Bayern Munich visited Ibrox. The influence of Graeme Souness was apparent in the team's performance and despite losing 2–0 to two late West German goals, the huge crowd left Ibrox that night enthusing over the type of football Rangers had played. There was a studied, flowing approach about it and the players were encouraged to pass the ball around as much as possible. It was very much Graeme Souness, very much Liverpool and very much liked by the fans!

Souness had stated publicly that he didn't expect to win the title in his first season at the helm, but that couldn't stop the natural optimism of the Rangers supporters as the start of the season approached. The events of Saturday, 9 August, caused many of them to change their views.

Graeme Souness's first taste of the Premier League was against Hibs at Easter Road and it lasted just thirty-seven minutes. That was how long he was on the field before being sent-off following an appalling mêlée in the middle of the pitch, which at one stage involved almost every player from either side. Souness deeply regretted the dismissal, for a kick at Hibs striker George McCluskey, and admitted later that he should have known better than to fall into the trap set for the big-spending, high-profile player–manager of Rangers.

Souness was suspended from the next League match, a 1–0 win over Falkirk at Ibrox, which reaped two much needed points following the 2–1 defeat at Easter Road. Northern Ireland international full-back Jimmy Nicholl made his second 'début' for Rangers in the win, following the swap deal which brought him back to Ibrox with striker Bobby Williamson making the opposite journey to West Bromwich Albion.

Rangers overcame their rough start, which included throwing away a 2–0 lead to lose to Dundee United at Ibrox, and their progress was steady if unspectacular.

Serving a three-match suspension imposed by the Scottish Football Association, Souness had to watch the first 'Old Firm' clash of the season from the stand as Celtic visited Ibrox for a live TV encounter on Sunday, 31 August. It was crucial for Rangers that their rivals shouldn't gain any further ground on them so early in the season and Ian Durrant scored the only goal of the match to round off a splendid performance by the Light Blues. They were looking good, making progress in the Skol Cup and showing signs of real consistency in the championship race.

The playing-staff continued to be changed, strikers Iain Ferguson and John MacDonald moving to Dundee United and Barnsley respectively, with Ally

McCoist and Robert Fleck forming a productive partnership in the first-team following a bad injury sustained by Colin West in a Skol Cup tie against East Fife.

Fleck scored a hat-trick, his second in the space of four days, as Rangers began their UEFA Cup campaign with a 4–0 win over the Finnish side Ilves Tampere at Ibrox.

Ted McMinn, the completely unpredictable winger, was also enjoying a rich vein of form and was instrumental in the progress to the Skol Cup final, scoring a brilliant individual goal in the 2–1 semi-final success against Dundee United.

A thigh injury aggravated in the second-round UEFA Cup tie against Boavista Porto ruled Graeme Souness out of the Skol Cup show-down with Celtic at Hampden on Sunday, 26 October. He was a frustrated spectator once more as his players defeated their greatest rivals 2–1 with goals from Ian Durrant and Davie Cooper to give Souness his first major trophy as Rangers boss.

A Derek Ferguson twenty-yarder in Portugal took the team into the third round of Europe where they met Borussia Moenchengladbach. A 1–1 draw at Ibrox was followed by a goalless draw in West Germany where Rangers were bitterly upset at the dismissals of Stuart Munro and Davie Cooper. The away goals defeat was a blow, but by now Graeme Souness had his sights set on the League Championship. He realized it could be won at the first attempt, but he needed one more signing to tip the balance in Rangers' favour.

Graham Roberts duly arrived from Spurs for £450,000 on 21 December and he immediately won the hearts and minds of the Rangers supporters with a superb début performance against Dundee United at Ibrox, which was won 2–0. Roberts went on to form a formidable partnership with Terry Butcher at the heart of the Rangers defence and the foundation for a League triumph had been well and truly laid.

Another striker was added to the squad when young Neil Woods signed from Doncaster Rovers in a deal worth £150,000, which saw defenders Stuart Beattie and Colin Miller joining the Belle Vue club.

New Year's Day 1987 was crunch time for Rangers. They had successfully cut down Celtic's lead in the Championship, which at one juncture had stood at eight points, but knew that victory over the Parkhead men was crucial on Ne'erday at Ibrox.

The victory, by 2–0, came more easily than any of the Rangers fans could have hoped or expected. The Light Blues were in total control throughout, McCoist and Fleck providing the goals, while Graeme Souness was outstanding, dominating an 'Old Firm' match like no Rangers player had since the halcyon days of Jim Baxter.

Rangers now had the initiative in the title chase, but they didn't rest on their laurels, with Graeme Souness pruning his first-team squad further with the sales of midfielder Dougie Bell to Hibs, former captain Craig Paterson to Motherwell and supporters' favourite Ted McMinn to Seville following disciplinary problems with the winger. It was a clear indication of how firmly in charge Graeme Souness was and his coaching staff were now complete around him, long-serving Peter McCloy and former Anfield team-mate Phil Boersma making up a quartet.

A 2–0 win over Hamilton Accies at Ibrox on 17 January took Rangers to the top of the Premier League and they hadn't conceded a goal since Uwe Rahn scored for Borussia Moenchengladbach at Ibrox on 26 November. Chris Woods set a new British record for the longest run of consecutive shut-outs, but the spell was broken in a match which attracted screaming headlines in the newspapers.

Graeme Souness's first venture into the Scottish Cup was a third-round tie against Hamilton, rooted to the bottom of the Premier League, at Ibrox on 31 January. Although Woods duly chalked up the record of 1,196 minutes without conceding a goal during the match, his run was also broken when Hamilton full-back Adrian Sprott scored the only goal of the game in the seventieth minute. It was a stunning blow for Rangers and the dreams of a magical 'treble' in Graeme Souness's first season at the helm were gone. How would Rangers react to such a setback?

The answer came crystal clear the following Saturday when Rangers travelled to Edinburgh and crushed Hearts 5–2 at Tynecastle. It was a superb performance and it ended the Gorgie club's long unbeaten home run. With the prolific Ally McCoist maintaining his freescoring form, notably with a hat-trick in the 3–1 win over St Mirren at Love Street, the Ibrox men marched to a commanding position at the top of the Championship table by the end of February.

If there were any doubts about their Championship credentials, they were swept aside in March as five straight wins were recorded in the Premier League, which included a devastating 4–0 win over Dundee at Dens Park, a venue long regarded as something of a jinx ground for Rangers. The consistency was superb and it was a measure of how resilient the side were that they were able to shrug aside a 3–1 defeat against Celtic at Parkhead at the start of April and go through the rest of the month unbeaten to put their first title since 1978 within their grasp.

The glorious day that the Rangers fans had waited for was 2 May 1987 – a marvellous occasion never to be forgotten as a new generation of the club's supporters saw their heroes become champions.

It was a tough assignment as Rangers travelled north to take on Aberdeen at Pittodrie, needing two points from a ground where they had not won since 1982 to be sure of the title. Thousands of Rangers supporters, many without tickets, made the trek towards the Northern Lights, certain in the knowledge that this was to be the day when their brightest dreams were fulfilled.

It all seemed to be turning into a nightmare when Graeme Souness was sent off by referee Jim Duncan in the first half, but Rangers showed no sign of handicap with ten men and they took the lead with a goal which is certain to become a part of Ibrox legend. Davie Cooper swung over a free-kick from the left and it was supremely fitting that Terry Butcher should rise majestically to power an unstoppable header past Jim Leighton's right hand into the net.

The joy of the Rangers supporters was unrestrained, but Aberdeen subdued

131

Opposite HAPPY CAPTAIN Terry Butcher holds aloft the League Cup after Rangers 2–1 Hampden win over Celtic in October 1986 which gave Graeme Souness his first major trophy with the club.

Above THE ENGLISH CONNECTION Terry Butcher, Chris Woods and Graham Roberts, the three Anglos who played a crucial role in the 1986–87 Premier League triumph, celebrate with the fans at Ibrox.

Left WE HAVE LIFT OFF Ally McCoist leaps high on the shoulders of Robert Fleck after the little striker had scored the late equalizer in the 1987–88 Skol Cup final. McCoist and Fleck shared sixty-four goals in the previous season's title triumph.

the party on the stroke of half-time when Brian Irvine stabbed in the equalizer following a desperate goalmouth scramble. The Ibrox men held on in the second half and suddenly the news filtered through that Celtic were losing 2–1 to Falkirk at Parkhead. When the final whistle blew, Rangers were the champions.

The supporters spilled on to the pitch, their pent-up emotions released and the celebrations starting in earnest. It was a fantastic achievement for Graeme Souness, tempered by his dismissal in the clinching match, but he joined the lap of honour and deservedly accepted the acclaim of the fans along with Walter Smith. The Premier League trophy was presented to Terry Butcher at Ibrox the following Saturday when a capacity crowd enjoyed a gala day in the final match of the season against St Mirren, with Robert Fleck scoring the only goal of the game.

The success of 1986–87 was greater than anyone could have expected and it was clearly going to be a hard act to follow in 1987–88. With the added spice of a European Cup campaign to come, Graeme Souness immediately set about restructuring his squad and he purchased former Liverpool team-mate Avi Cohen from Maccabi Tel Aviv for £100,000 and snapped up John McGregor from Liverpool on a free transfer. Midfield man Bobby Russell was handed a free transfer and joined Motherwell and Souness completed his pre-season dealings by bringing striker Mark Falco to Ibrox from Watford for a fee of £270,000. Despite the 64-goal partnership enjoyed by Robert Fleck and Ally McCoist, a big bustling striker of Falco's kind was seen as the ideal foil for McCoist and that was the pairing which started the new season.

A pre-season trip to Switzerland and West Germany allowed Souness to try out his new ideas and although there was an appalling 5–0 defeat at the hands of FC Zurich, the team got their act together to finish the tour with an impressive 2–0 win over Bayer Uerdingen.

Striker Neil Woods, who had never settled at Ibrox owing to an unfortunate injury, was off-loaded to Ipswich Town for £125,000 as the changes continued and former captain and experienced defender Ally Dawson moved to Blackburn Rovers for £50,000.

Rangers knew they would be without Graham Roberts, Terry Butcher and Graeme Souness for the first two matches of the season through suspension and, as expected, the trio were badly missed as the campaign got underway with a dropped point at home to Dundee United and a 1–0 defeat against Hibs at Easter Road. When Aberdeen beat the Light Blues 2–0 at Pittodrie in the third League match of the season, they were already five points behind Celtic and Hearts and that immediately looked like a big gap to bridge. Their league form was nowhere near as consistent as it had been the previous season and when Graeme Souness was sent-off at Parkhead in the first 'Old Firm' clash of the term, Billy Stark scoring the only goal of the game, things looked bleak.

At least Rangers were able to encourage and excite their fans with good progress in the Skol and European Cups. They reserved their most impressive performances for the Skol Cup, and one 4–1 win over Hearts at Ibrox was as good as anything the team had produced under the leadership of Graeme Souness.

The first round of the European Cup had given Rangers the toughest task imaginable – they had to take on the might of Dynamo Kiev, the Russian champions rated by many as the finest club side in the world at the time and virtually the Soviet national team *en bloc*.

The Light Blues showed magnificent maturity and discipline when they travelled to the Ukraine for the first leg of the tie, a total of 100,000 people watching as Rangers defended superbly to hold Dynamo to a 1–0 win in the Republic Stadium.

By the time the second leg came around, Rangers were already into the final of the Skol Cup and Graeme Souness had again been busy in the transfer market. Striker Colin West was sold to Sheffield Wednesday for £150,000 while winger Ian McCall arrived in a £200,000 deal from Dunfermline and experienced English forward Trevor Francis was captured from Atalanta in Italy for just £75,000.

It was a marvellous night on 30 September 1987 for the Rangers supporters who packed into Ibrox for the second leg of the battle against Dynamo Kiev as they saw their heroes conjure up a memorable and inspiring display to overcome the Russians. A dreadful error from goalkeeper Viktor Chanov allowed Mark Falco to level the aggregate scores with a first-half goal and as the teams lined up for the second half, there was a tremendous air of anticipation around Ibrox.

The atmosphere was absolutely electric and even experienced players like Graeme Souness, Trevor Francis and Terry Butcher admitted afterwards that they had never experienced anything like the volume of noise inside the stadium that night. It reached a massive crescendo early in the second half when Francis swung the ball over from the right, Falco headed it back across goal and Ally McCoist directed his header past the despairing reach of Chanov to put Rangers 2–0 in front. That was the final outcome and Rangers had eliminated one of Europe's top sides from the tournament.

Sadly, Rangers' fortunes in the Premier League continued to be inconsistent and the 'Old Firm' match at Ibrox on 17 October was dramatic in the extreme with Chris Woods and Terry Butcher being sent-off along with Celtic's Frank McAvennie. Rangers fought back from 2–0 down to grab a point with a last-minute equalizer from Richard Gough, but in the final analysis it was a point dropped in the struggle to retain their title.

Gough had been bought from Spurs for a record fee of £1.1 million earlier that month and on Sunday, 25 October, he helped Rangers win the Skol Cup yet again in a magnificent final against Aberdeen. Hampden had not seen a game like it for many a year as Rangers fought back from losing an early penalty-kick to lead 2–1 with superb goals scored by Davie Cooper and Ian Durrant. The pendulum swung again when Aberdeen scored twice to lead 3–2 in the closing stages, but Rangers were not to be denied and it was Robert Fleck who took the match into extra-time with a dramatic equalizer. There was no further scoring and a nail-biting penalty shoot-out was needed to separate the sides. Aberdeen midfielder Peter Nicholas skied his kick over the crossbar and it was left to Ian Durrant to slot the decisive penalty past Jim Leighton to win the trophy for Rangers.

There seemed to be real light emerging for the club at that stage and Rangers reached the quarter-finals of the European Cup with a 4–2 aggregate win over Polish champions Gornik Zabrze. Disaster struck, however, on 17 November at Ibrox when captain Terry Butcher broke his left leg in an accidental clash with Aberdeen defender Alex McLeish. The injury would have severe consequences and although Rangers maintained their League challenge, it suffered a blow on 2 January 1988 when Celtic won the 'Old Firm' meeting at Parkhead 2–0.

By that time, there had been more frantic activity in the transfer market with strikers Mark Falco and Robert Fleck both leaving Ibrox for English football with Queen's Park Rangers (£350,000) and Norwich City (£580,000) respectively. Joining the club were midfielder Ray Wilkins for £150,000 from Paris St Germain and exciting winger Mark Walters from Aston Villa for £500,000. Graeme Souness flew to Paris and persuaded England star Wilkins to sign for Rangers within a couple of hours, while Walters became the first black player to appear in the Premier Division. Both players made favourable impressions on the supporters as did midfielder John Brown, recruited from Dundee for £350,000 in January and Danish international defender Jan Bartram who was snapped up for £180,000 from Silkeborg.

Rangers embarked on an eight-match unbeaten run after that defeat by Celtic early in the year, but it was brought to an abrupt end on 20 February when Dunfermline sent them tumbling from the Scottish Cup with a 2–0 win at East End Park in the fourth-round tie.

With the Premier League seemingly swinging away in Celtic's favour, the European Cup now offered Rangers their greatest chance of real glory in the season and the quarter-final tie against Steaua Bucharest took on even greater significance.

Ian Ferguson, St Mirren's prodigious young midfield star, was finally captured at a cost of £750,000 but his move came too late for him to play any role in the matches against the Rumanian champions.

Rangers got off to a disastrous start in the first leg in Bucharest when Victor Piturca gave Steaua a second-minute lead and although they defended well for the rest of the match, an unlucky deflection saw Stefan Iovan's free-kick beat Chris Woods in the sixty-sixth minute to give the Rumanians a 2–0 lead to take to Ibrox.

A capacity crowd gave Graeme Souness and his men all the backing they could have wished for, even after a defensive error in the second minute again gave Steaua an early goal with Marius Lacatus the marksman. It now seemed a lost cause for Rangers but they gave their fans their money's worth and by half-time were 2–1 ahead on the night and just 3–2 down on aggregate. Richard Gough and Ally McCoist scored the goals, but despite a policy of all-out attack in the second half, they couldn't breach the Steaua defence again and the European dream was over. Any chances of overtaking Celtic in the Premier League race were smashed at Ibrox four days later on 20 March when Billy McNeill's side won a crucial fixture 2–1. It was a stark contrast from the end of the previous season and Celtic went on to regain the Championship.

REAL SKOLARS The victorious Rangers squad after their thrilling Skol League Cup triumph against Aberdeen at Hampden in 1987–88. *Back row*: Ally McCoist, Derek Ferguson, Richard Gough, Jimmy Nicholl, Ian Durrant, John McGregor, Davie Cooper. *Front Row*: Stuart Munro, Graham Roberts, Trevor Francis, Avi Cohen, Nicky Walker, Robert Fleck.

KING RICHARD Richard Gough became Rangers biggest buy to date when he came to Ibrox from Tottenham Hotspur for £1,100,000 in October 1987. Here he breaks up an Aberdeen attack during the 1987–88 Skol Cup final.

MARK WALTERS   One of the most exciting talents to arrive in Scotland, Mark became the first black player to perform in the Premier League. His £500,000 fee to Aston Villa in January 1988 is proving to be a bargain.

With the Scottish Cup joining the Premier League trophy on the Parkhead sideboard, it was more than evident that Celtic had picked up the gauntlet thrown down by the arrival of Graeme Souness at Ibrox. Their success had taken Rangers by surprise and made the disappointments of 1987–88 all the harder to take. The Light Blues support would now demand an even greater response from their heroes. No one needed to inform Graeme Souness of that fact and he quickly began planning to recapture the prize he values most of all – the Premier League title.

Delighted to put the season behind them, Rangers faced 1988–89 minus the services of defenders Graham Roberts and Jan Bartram, both leaving under a cloud.

Roberts, a hugely popular player with the Rangers supporters, signed for Chelsea for £475,000. It was an inevitable departure, Roberts's dressing-room fall-out with Graeme Souness following the last home match of the season having been made public. Having challenged the authority of the Rangers manager, Roberts knew that his exit had to come. Souness made it plain to everyone who was in charge.

Bartram's brief stay at Ibrox ended when he returned to Denmark, signing for Brondby in a £315,000 deal. His departure too was in many ways inevitable after controversial interviews he had given to the Danish press were enthusiastically and sensationally reproduced in Scotland. It was quite clear that the Dane didn't relish the physical nature of Scottish football and few Rangers fans were disappointed at his loss – they were more concerned at how Roberts would be replaced.

Graeme Souness was certainly in no mood to be idle in the transfer market and he started off by buying a striker, Kevin Drinkell, from Norwich City for £500,000. The arrival of the 28-year-old Englishman raised more than a few eyebrows but Rangers had been watching him for some time and were convinced that they had at last found the perfect foil for Ally McCoist.

Souness led his first-team squad to Italy for pre-season training, a change in routine which he hoped would be the first stage of a successful season. The idyllic Il Ciocco complex near Pisa was the location for the Ibrox players but there would be no basking in the sunshine. On the contrary, they had ten days of the hardest training experienced by Rangers for years with Graeme Souness and Walter Smith watching the players' efforts approvingly. The decision not to go on the more traditional pre-season tour in Europe, playing five or six matches, was a calculated one which surprised many people.

Midway through their stay in Italy, Rangers were joined by England international right-back Gary Stevens. Souness had swooped to sign him from Everton in a £1,000,000 deal which took his total spending at Ibrox to over £7 million. Stevens had made his name as a pacy, attacking defender and his arrival gave some hint of what Souness had planned for the new season.

Equally as important as any new signing for Rangers would be the success or otherwise of Terry Butcher's return from injury. The broken leg had not healed in time for the Rangers captain to play again before the end of the 1987–88 season and he was also forced to withdraw from the summer European

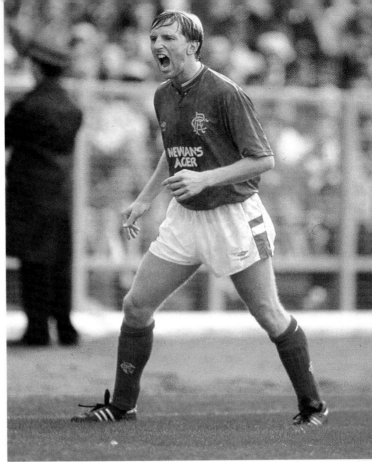

Above left MEL STERLAND Graeme Souness took his spending on players at Ibrox to over £8 million when he signed Sterland from Sheffield Wednesday for £800,000 in March 1989. The defender or midfielder quickly repaid his new manager, scoring two spectacular goals in the title-clinching 4–0 win over Hearts at Ibrox the following month.

Above right GARY STEVENS Rangers' second £1 million signing when Graeme Souness paid that amount to Everton for him in July 1988. A regular in the England international team, the attacking right-back slotted comfortably into the Ibrox defence alongside fellow Englishmen Chris Woods and Terry Butcher.

Left RAY WILKINS Classy and elegant midfield veteran who enjoyed a star-studded career with Chelsea, Manchester United and A C Milan. Snapped up by Rangers for just £150,000 from Paris St Germain, the 84-times capped Englishman was a huge influence in the 1988–89 championship triumph.

Opposite IAN FERGUSON After the difficulty of his initial settling-in period, Ferguson showed exactly why Rangers paid St Mirren £850,000 for his services. His power play from midfield brought him superb goals for Rangers, hero-worship from the supporters and full international caps for Scotland.

Championship Finals in West Germany. He had been as badly missed by England there as he was by Rangers and all eyes were on Butcher as he lined up in the unglamorous setting of Starks Park, Kirkcaldy on Saturday, 30 July.

Raith Rovers were the opponents in Rangers' opening challenge match of the season and the game against the First Division side represented Butcher's first public examination. He came through it well and if he naturally had some pace to recover, he put in enough full-blooded challenges to delight the Rangers support as the game was won 2–1.

The Light Blues proceeded to cruise through a carefully prepared warm-up programme which was concluded with a 3–1 win over French side Bordeaux at Ibrox in Davie Cooper's testimonial match.

Rangers looked fit and ready for the challenges ahead and began their title bid with a comfortable 2–0 win against promoted Hamilton Accies at Douglas Park. Gary Stevens began his Premier League career with a goal and the other came from the head of Ally McCoist. The confidence of the players transmitted itself to the supporters and by the end of August the fans were in no doubt that they were about to witness a glorious season.

Rangers charged to the top of the table, dropping just one point in their opening eight League fixtures. The undoubted highlight in that run was the first 'Old Firm' game of the season which turned out to be one of the most remarkable in the long series of clashes between the rivals.

Ibrox was the venue and 27 August the date. No Rangers fan present will ever forget it while the Celtic supporters will wish they could. The Light Blues romped to a 5–1 victory and that after going behind in the opening minutes to a goal scored by Frank McAvennie. Rangers' response was furious and stylish. Ally McCoist equalized and then Ray Wilkins earned a 2–1 interval advantage with a thunderous volley from twenty-two yards which has rarely been bettered at Ibrox. McCoist made it 3–1 a minute after the restart and Celtic could do little to stem the Rangers tidal wave. Goals from Kevin Drinkell, quickly proving a favourite with the fans, and Mark Walters completed a rout that could have been even greater.

It was a difficult task for Graeme Souness to quench the euphoria which naturally surrounded Rangers after that game but he was successful in doing so and the team settled down to some consistent form which swept their opponents aside.

They stormed into the Skol Cup Final, scoring sixteen goals in their four matches *en route* to another showdown against Aberdeen. Helping them on their way was veteran striker Andy Gray, signed from West Bromwich Albion for just £25,000 in September.

Born and raised in Drumchapel, Gray was a self-confessed Rangers fan and could scarcely believe it when Graeme Souness offered him the chance to play for the Light Blues. The former Scotland star was brought in as cover for Kevin Drinkell and Ally McCoist as both strikers suffered injuries at various stages of the season.

Rangers took their unbeaten run in all matches to fourteen games and it came to an end in bitter circumstances at Pittodrie on 8 October. Neale Cooper, making his début following his £250,000 capture from Aston Villa, opened the scoring against his former club but Aberdeen hit back to win 2–1, Charlie Nicholas heading the winner in the closing minutes.

Of more concern to Graeme Souness was the injury sustained in the match by midfielder Ian Durrant. The youngster suffered damaged cruciate ligaments on his right knee in a tackle from Dons' midfielder Neil Simpson which shocked all who witnessed it. Souness could barely contain his anger afterwards and a stunned Durrant found himself in hospital with the realization he would not play again in 1988–89. The barrage of cards and flowers from the Rangers support showed the esteem they had for Durrant, one of Scotland's finest young players.

Rangers had to put their dismay behind them and prepare for the Skol Cup Final on Sunday, 23 October. Ironically, the Hampden date was against Aberdeen but Graeme Souness appealed for no vendettas and hoped for a repeat of the previous season's classic final between the sides.

That's exactly what an enthralled crowd of 72,122 at Hampden witnessed along with those who watched the game live on television.

Rangers lifted the trophy for the third successive season, winning the tournament for the sixteenth time in all, and gave Graeme Souness his fourth domestic triumph out of seven competitions played for since his arrival.

Twice Rangers were ahead in the game, first through Ally McCoist's penalty and then through a spectacular volley by Ian Ferguson. On both occasions, Aberdeen hit back to equalize with goals from Davie Dodds. There was frenetic goalmouth incident at both ends of the pitch in the closing minutes but it was that man McCoist who popped up to clinch a thrilling 3–2 victory for Rangers.

It was a triumphant start to the domestic campaign and the more optimistic Rangers fans were already talking about the prospects of their team winning the 'treble'. Graeme Souness dismissed that and continued to state that the Premier League was the most important piece of silverware for him in this or any other season.

On the European front, Rangers made a disappointing exit in the second round of the U E F A Cup at the hands of a Cologne side who were far from formidable.

Having beaten Polish team G K S Katowice 5–2 on aggregate in the first round, Rangers travelled to West Germany two days after their Skol Cup success confident of doing well against Cologne. That confidence did not look misplaced as the Light Blues created and missed the best chances of the match in the Mungersdorff Stadium, only to capitulate badly in the final fifteen minutes and lose 2–0.

The second leg at Ibrox saw Rangers produce plenty of passion and commitment in front of a crowd willing them to pull back the deficit but the task proved too much and Kevin Drinkell's superb headed goal in the 1–1 draw was in vain.

Ally McCoist was on the sidelines for the match, having been out of action with a hamstring injury sustained at Love Street on 29 October. It was a strain which would prove worse than at first thought and the striker did not return to action until 21 January.

Left KEVIN DRINKELL A powerful striker who matches tremendous workrate with good skill in the air and on the ground. Signed from Norwich City for £500,000 in June 1988, he quickly became a favourite with the Rangers supporters.

Below CHAMPIONS Jubilant Rangers players celebrate in the Ibrox dressing-room after beating Hearts 4–0 on 29 April 1989 to clinch the Premier League title. It was the club's 39th championship and fitting reward for twelve months of preparation and planning by Graeme Souness.

Another blow came in the shape of illness to Chris Woods. The big goalkeeper was struck down by the mysterious labyrinthitis, an affliction which affects balance and vision. He was out of commission from 16 November to 18 February and Rangers' resources were stretched at a crucial stage of the season.

They maintained their lead at the top of the Premier League, despite losing two successive matches for the first time in the season, to Dundee United and Hearts, in December. Mark Walters, Ian Ferguson and Andy Gray improvised up front along with Kevin Drinkell while Nicky Walker proved as able a deputy as ever for Chris Woods.

The supporters were certainly not complaining when Rangers got the New Year off to the perfect start with a 4–1 win over Celtic at Ibrox. Having lost 3–1 at Parkhead in November, the Light Blues were keen for a repeat of their August joy day against their greatest rivals and they almost matched it perfectly.

Again Celtic opened the scoring, this time through Chris Morris, but Rangers stormed back with goals from Mark Walters (two), Terry Butcher and Ian Ferguson sending the Light Blue legions home in a state of uncontained joy.

If that was the most significant occurrence on the pitch, Rangers were as ever making news behind the scenes. They had stunned the media and public yet again when the club found itself with a new owner on 23 November 1988.

The end of an era spanning thirty-four years came when Lawrence Marlborough sold his controlling interest in Rangers Football Club to millionaire businessman David Murray. The grandson of John Lawrence, former chairman of the club, Marlborough had been responsible for putting David Holmes at the helm of the Ibrox ship to bring Graeme Souness to Glasgow.

Business commitments in the United States finally led Marlborough to transfer control of Rangers to a man he felt sure he could trust with the future of the stadium, team and supporters.

That man was Murray, at thirty-six one of Britain's most successful businessmen. He lost both legs in a car crash in 1976 but his disability served only to make him even more determined to succeed. By the time he bought Rangers, his company employed 1,000 people and expected profits of £6 million for 1988.

Murray's friendship with Graeme Souness was the major factor in the sale and suddenly Souness became a director of the club, financially committing himself to a 10 per cent share in the club to increase his power and profile at Ibrox.

Still, regaining the Premier League title remained as Souness's priority and following a hiccup against Motherwell at Fir Park on 7 January, his team began a twelve-match unbeaten run which would bring the flag back to Ibrox.

One by one, challengers Dundee United, Celtic and Aberdeen fell by the wayside and the most significant result, almost inevitably, came in an 'Old Firm' match.

On 1 April 1989 Rangers recorded their first League win at Parkhead since 1980 and the two points gained left the title within touching distance. Kevin Drinkell and Ally McCoist scored the goals in a 2–1 win which formally ended Celtic's quest to retain their title.

Aberdeen kept up the chase longest but the glory day finally came at Ibrox on 29 April. Hearts provided little resistance as Rangers clinched the championship in true style with a 4–0 win which delighted the jubilant support.

Souness's most recent signings both made contributions on the day. Mel Sterland, an £800,000 capture from Sheffield Wednesday, scored two superb goals while teenager Tom Cowan, snapped up from Clyde for £100,000, gave the fans a hint of what the future held.

Kevin Drinkell matched Sterland's double on a day when Rangers fielded no fewer than seven Englishmen in their starting line-up, a sign of the extent of the Souness revolution at Ibrox.

The manager stated afterwards that he had never wanted to win anything so much in his illustrious career as he had this particular championship.

Rangers' success had also been translated to the Scottish Cup at last, a competition which held nothing but bad memories for Souness. Early exits at the hands of Hamilton and Dunfermline in his first two seasons ensured that.

This time, the Light Blues made it to the final for the first time since 1983, despite requiring replays to eliminate Raith Rovers, Dundee United and St Johnstone. In each of those ties, Rangers had produced enough style in the second games to convince their fans that the historic 'treble' was a real prospect.

Blocking their path to the fifth 'treble' in the club's history were Celtic, desperate to salvage something from a season which mirrored the disappointment suffered by Rangers in 1987–88.

Graeme Souness did not have his troubles to seek as the Hampden date approached and when the teams took the field on 20 May, there was no Ray Wilkins nor Derek Ferguson in the Rangers midfield. Both had failed to recover from injuries in time and the Light Blues were without a playmaker in the Cup Final. Wilkins's absence was a particularly bad blow as the veteran Englishman had been an outstanding contributor to the success of the team throughout the season.

Souness reshuffled his pack and included himself as a substitute. The game was a huge disappointment, Rangers losing a scrappy contest to the only goal of the game four minutes from half-time. Joe Miller pounced on a loose pass back by Gary Stevens and try as they might, Rangers could not force their way back into the match despite creating the opportunities to do so as they pressed forward in the closing stages.

When referee Bob Valentine, an enormously unpopular figure with the Rangers fans, disallowed a headed 'goal' from Terry Butcher in the dying minutes, it was clear that the dreams of the treble were over. The natural disappointment was soon tempered by the manager as he pointed out what had been achieved during the season. Rangers were heading back into the European Cup and, as he never tires of saying, that Premier League title means more than anything to him.

David Murray, the man charged with leading Rangers into the 1990s and beyond, perhaps best summed up the mood at the end of 1988–89 when he said: 'This club has a lot to look back upon and a whole lot more to look forward to.'

As John Allan wrote all those years ago, the story of the Rangers is indeed one that's worth telling. There is much more yet to be revealed . . .

RANGERS RECORDS

RANGERS SCOTTISH LEAGUE RECORD, 1890–91 to 1988–89

FIRST DIVISION

Season	P	W	D	L	F	A	Pts.	Psn.
1890–91	18	13	3	2	58	25	29	1st*
1891–92	22	12	2	8	57	49	26	4th
1892–93	18	12	4	2	41	27	28	2nd
1893–94	18	8	4	6	44	30	20	4th
1894–95	18	10	2	6	41	26	22	3rd
1895–96	18	11	4	3	57	39	26	2nd
1896–97	18	11	3	4	64	30	25	3rd
1897–98	18	13	3	2	71	15	29	2nd
1898–99	18	18	0	0	79	18	36	1st
1899–1900	18	15	2	1	69	27	32	1st
1900–01	20	17	1	2	60	25	35	1st
1901–02	22	11	2	9	59	46	24	1st
1902–03	22	12	5	5	56	30	29	3rd
1903–04	26	16	6	4	80	33	38	4th
1904–05	26	19	3	4	83	28	41	2nd†
1905–06	30	15	7	8	58	48	37	4th
1906–07	34	19	7	8	69	33	45	3rd
1907–08	34	21	8	5	74	40	50	3rd
1908–09	34	19	7	8	91	38	45	4th
1909–10	34	20	6	8	70	35	46	3rd
1910–11	34	23	6	5	90	34	52	1st
1911–12	34	24	3	7	86	34	51	1st
1912–13	34	24	5	5	76	41	53	1st
1913–14	38	27	5	6	79	31	59	2nd
1914–15	38	23	4	11	74	47	50	3rd
1915–16	38	25	6	7	87	39	56	2nd
1916–17	38	24	5	9	68	32	53	3rd
1917–18	34	25	6	3	66	24	56	1st
1918–19	34	26	5	3	86	16	57	2nd
1919–20	42	31	9	2	106	25	71	1st
1920–21	42	35	6	1	91	24	76	1st
1921–22	42	28	10	4	83	26	66	2nd
1922–23	38	23	9	6	67	29	55	1st
1923–24	38	25	9	4	72	22	59	1st
1924–25	38	25	10	3	77	27	60	1st
1925–26	38	19	6	13	79	55	44	6th
1926–27	38	23	10	5	85	41	56	1st
1927–28	38	26	8	4	109	36	60	1st
1928–29	38	30	7	1	107	32	67	1st
1929–30	38	28	4	6	94	32	60	1st
1930–31	38	27	6	5	96	29	60	1st
1931–32	38	28	5	5	118	42	61	2nd
1932–33	38	26	10	2	113	43	62	1st
1933–34	38	30	6	2	118	41	66	1st
1934–35	38	25	5	8	96	46	55	1st
1935–36	38	27	7	4	110	43	61	2nd
1936–37	38	26	9	3	88	32	61	1st
1937–38	38	18	13	7	75	49	49	3rd
1938–39	38	25	9	4	112	55	59	1st
1946–47	30	21	4	5	76	26	46	1st
1947–48	30	21	4	5	64	28	46	2nd
1948–49	30	20	6	4	63	32	46	1st
1949–50	30	22	6	2	58	26	50	1st
1950–51	30	17	4	9	64	37	38	2nd
1951–52	30	16	9	5	61	31	41	2nd
1952–53	30	18	7	5	80	39	43	1st
1953–54	30	13	8	9	56	35	34	4th
1954–55	30	19	3	8	67	33	41	3rd
1955–56	34	22	8	4	85	27	52	1st
1956–57	34	26	3	5	96	48	55	1st
1957–58	34	22	5	7	89	49	49	2nd
1958–59	34	21	8	5	92	51	50	1st
1959–60	34	17	8	9	72	38	42	3rd
1960–61	34	23	5	6	88	46	51	1st
1961–62	34	22	7	5	84	31	51	2nd
1962–63	34	25	7	2	94	28	57	1st
1963–64	34	25	5	4	85	31	55	1st
1964–65	34	18	8	8	78	35	44	5th
1965–66	34	25	5	4	91	29	55	2nd
1966–67	34	24	7	3	92	31	55	2nd
1967–68	34	28	5	1	93	34	61	2nd
1968–69	34	21	7	6	81	32	49	2nd
1969–70	34	19	7	8	67	40	45	2nd
1970–71	34	16	9	9	58	34	41	4th
1971–72	34	21	2	11	71	38	44	3rd
1972–73	34	26	4	4	74	30	56	2nd
1973–74	34	21	6	7	67	34	48	3rd
1974–75	34	25	6	3	86	33	56	1st

PREMIER DIVISION

Season	P	W	D	L	F	A	Pts.	Psn.
1975–76	36	23	8	5	59	24	54	1st
1976–77	36	18	10	8	62	37	46	2nd
1977–78	36	24	7	5	76	39	55	1st
1978–79	36	18	9	9	52	35	45	2nd
1979–80	36	15	7	14	50	46	37	5th
1980–81	36	16	12	8	60	32	44	3rd
1981–82	36	16	11	9	57	45	43	3rd
1982–83	36	13	12	11	52	41	38	4th
1983–84	36	15	12	9	53	41	42	4th
1984–85	36	13	12	11	47	38	38	4th
1985–86	36	13	9	14	53	45	35	5th
1986–87	44	31	7	6	85	23	69	1st
1987–88	44	26	8	10	85	34	60	3rd
1988–89	36	26	4	6	62	26	56	1st

* Finished level on points with Dumbarton, Rangers drew play-off match 2–2 and were declared joint Champions.
† Finished level on points with Celtic but lost play-off.

RANGERS SCOTTISH CUP RECORD

1873–74
Did not compete

1874–75
Round 1
v Oxford (a) 2–0
Round 2
v Dumbarton (h) 0–0
Replay
v Dumbarton (a) 0–1

1875–76
Round 1
v 1st L.R.V. (h) 7–0
Round 2
v Third Lanark (h) 1–2

1876–77
Round 1
v Queen's Park Juniors (h) 4–1
Round 2
v Towerhill (a) 8–0
Round 3
Bye
Round 4
v Mauchline (a) 3–0
Round 5
v Lennox (a) 3–0
Semi-final
Bye
Final
v Vale of Leven (Hamilton Cres.) 1–1
Replay
v Vale of Leven (Hamilton Cres.) 1–1
Second Replay
v Vale of Leven (H*) 2–3
* H = Hampden Park

1877–78
Round 1
v Possilpark (h) 13–0
Round 2
v Alexandra Athletic (h) 8–0
Round 3
v Uddington (h) 13–0
Round 4
v Vale of Leven (h) 0–0
Replay
v Vale of Leven (a) 0–5

1878–79
Round 1
v Shaftesbury (h) 3–0
Round 2
v Whitefield (a) 6–1

Round 3
v Parkgrove (h) 8–2
Round 4
v Alexandra Athletic (h) 3–0
Round 5
v Partick (h) 4–0
Round 6
v Queen's Park (a) 1–0
Semi-final
Bye
Final
v Vale of Leven (H) 1–1*
* A protest by Rangers on the ground that they had scored a second goal was not sustained by the SFA, and they declined to replay. Vale of Leven were, therefore, awarded the Cup.

1879–80
Round 1
v Queen's Park (h) 0–0
Replay
v Queen's Park (a) 1–5

1880–81
Round 1
v Govan (h) 4–1
Round 2
v Northern (a) 1–0
Round 3
v Partick Thistle (h) 3–0
Round 4
v Clyde (h) 11–0
Round 5
v Hurlford (a) 3–0
Round 6
v Dumbarton (h) 1–3

1881–82
Round 1
v Third Lanark (h) 2–1
Round 2
v Harmonic (Scratched) WO
Round 3
v Alexandra Athletic (h) 3–1
Round 4
v Thornliebank (a) 2–0
Round 5
v South Western (h) 4–0*
Round 6
v Dumbarton (a) 1–5†
* After a protested game, won by Rangers 2–1
† After a protested game

1882–83
Round 1
v Jordanhill (a) 4–0
Round 2
v Queen's Park (a) 2–3

1883–84
Round 1
v Northern (a) 1–0
Round 2
v Whitehill (h) 14–2
Round 3
v Falkirk (h) 5–2
Round 4
v Dunblane (a) 6–1
Round 5
v St Bernard (a) 3–0
Round 6
v Cambuslang (a) 5–1
Semi-final
v Vale of Leven (Alexandria) 0–3

1884–85
Round 1
v Whitehill (h) 11–0
Round 2
v Third Lanark (a) 2–2
Replay
v Third Lanark (h) 0–0
Second Replay
v Third Lanark (a) 3–0
Round 3
v Arbroath (a) 8–1*
Round 4
Bye
Round 5
v Renton (a) 3–5
* After protested game, which Arbroath won by 4–3

1885–86
Round 1
v Clyde (a) 0–1

1886–87
Round 1
v Govan Athletic (h) 9–1
Round 2
v Westbourne (h) 5–2
Round 3
v Cambuslang (h) 0–2

1887–88
Round 1
v Battlefield (h) 4–1
Round 2
v Partick Thistle (a) 1–2

1888–89
Round 1
v Partick Thistle (h) 4–2
Round 2
v Clyde (a) 2–2
Replay
v Clyde (h) 0–3

1889–90
Round 1
v United Abstainers (h) 6–2
Round 2
v Kelvinside Athletic (a)
13–0
Round 3
v Vale of Leven (h) 0–0
Replay
v Vale of Leven (a) 2–3

1890–91
Round 1
v Celtic (a) 0–1

1891–92
Round 1
v St Bernards (h) 5–1
Round 2
v Kilmarnock (h) 0–0
Replay
v Kilmarnock (a) 1–1
Replay
v Kilmarnock (Paisley) 3–2
Round 3
v Annbank (h) 2–0
Round 4
v Celtic (a) 3–5

1892–93
Round 1
v Annbank (h) 7–0
Round 2
v Dumbarton (a) 1–0
Round 3
v St Bernards (a) 2–3

1893–94
Round 1
v Cowlairs (h) 8–0
Round 2
v Leith Athletic (h) 2–0
Round 3
v Clyde (a) 5–0
Semi-final
v Queen's Park (h) 1–1
Replay
v Queen's Park (H) 3–1
Final
v Celtic (H) 3–1

1894–95
Round 1
v Heart of Midlothian (h)
1–2

1895–96
Round 1
v Dumbarton (a) 1–1
Replay
v Dumbarton (h) 3–1
Round 2
v St Mirren (h) 5–0

Round 3
v Hibernian (h) 2–3

1896–97
Round 1
v Partick Thistle (a) 4–2
Round 2
v Hibernian (h) 3–0
Round 3
v Dundee (a) 4–0
Semi-final
v Morton (a) 7–2
Final
v Dumbarton (H) 5–1

1897–98
Round 1
v Polton Vale (h) 8–0
Round 2
v Cartvale (h) 12–0
Round 3
v Queen's Park (h) 3–1
Semi-final
v Third Lanark (h) 1–1
Replay
v Third Lanark (a) 2–2
Replay
v Third Lanark (a) 2–0
Final
v Kilmarnock (H) 2–0

1898–99
Round 1
v Heart of Midlothian (h)
4–1
Round 2
v Ayr Parkhouse (a) 4–1
Round 3
v Clyde (h) 4–0
Semi-final
v St Mirren (a) 2–1
Final
v Celtic (H) 0–2

1899–1900
Round 1
v Morton (h) 4–2
Round 2
v Maybole (h) 12–0
Round 3
v Partick Thistle (a) 6–1
Semi-final
v Celtic (h) 2–2
Replay
v Celtic (a) 0–4

1900–01
Round 1
v Celtic (a) 0–1

1901–02
Round 1
v Johnstone (h) 6–1

Round 2
v Inverness Caledonian (h)
5–1
Round 3
v Kilmarnock (h) 2–0
Semi-final
v Hibernian (h) 0–2

1902–03
Round 1
v Auchterarder Thistle (h)
7–0
Round 2
v Kilmarnock (h) 4–0
Round 3
v Celtic (a) 3–0
Semi-final
v Stenhousemuir (a) 4–1
Final
v Heart of Midlothian
(Parkhead) 1–1
Replay
v Heart of Midlothian
(Parkhead) 0–0
Replay
v Heart of Midlothian
(Parkhead) 2–0

1903–04
Round 1
v Heart of Midlothian (h)
3–2
Round 2
v Hibernian (a) 2–1
Round 3
v St Mirren (a) 1–0
Semi-final
v Morton (h) 3–0
Final
v Celtic (H) 2–3

1904–05
Round 1
v Ayr Parkhouse (h) 2–1
Round 2
v Morton (a) 6–0
Round 3
v Beith (h) 5–1
Semi-final
v Celtic (a) 2–0
Final
v Third Lanark (H) 0–0
Replay
v Third Lanark (H) 1–3

1905–06
Round 1
v Arthurlie (a) 7–1
Round 2
v Aberdeen (a) 3–2
Round 3
v Port-Glasgow Ath. (a) 0–1

1906–07
Round 1
v Falkirk (a) 2–1
Round 2
v Galston (a) 4–0
Round 3
v Celtic (h) 0–3

1907–08
Round 1
v Falkirk (a) 2–2
Replay
v Falkirk (h) 4–1
Round 2
v Celtic (h) 1–2

1908–09
Round 1
v St Johnstone (a) 3–0
Round 2
v Dundee (a) 0–0
Replay
v Dundee (h) 1–0
Round 3
v Queen's Park (h) 1–0
Semi-final
v Falkirk (a) 1–0
Final
v Celtic (H) 2–2
Replay
v Celtic (H) 1–1
Cup withheld

1909–10
Round 1
v Inverness Thistle (h) 3–1
Round 2
v Clyde (a) 0–2

1910–11
Round 1
v Kilmarnock (h) 2–1
Round 2
v Morton (h) 3–0
Round 3
v Dundee (a) 1–2

1911–12
Round 1
v Stenhousemuir (h) 3–1
Round 2
v Clyde (a) 1–3

1912–13
Round 1
A Bye
Round 2
v Hamilton Acad. (a) 1–1
Replay
v Hamilton Acad. (h) 2–0
Round 3
v Falkirk (h) 1–3

1913–14
Round 1
A Bye
Round 2
v Alloa Athletic (h) 5–0
Round 3
v Hibernian (a) 1–2

1919–20
Round 1
v Dumbarton (h) 0–0
Replay
v Dumbarton (h) 1–0
Round 2
v Arbroath (h) 5–0
Round 3
v Broxburn United (h) 3–0
Round 4
v Celtic (h) 1–0
Semi-final
v Albion Rovers (Parkhead) 1–1
Replay
v Albion Rovers (Parkhead) 0–0
Replay
v Albion Rovers (Parkhead) 0–2

1920–21
Round 1
A Bye
Round 2
v Morton (h) 2–0
Round 3
v Alloa (h) 0–0
Replay
v Alloa (h) 4–1
Round 4
v Dumbarton (a) 3–0
Semi-final
v Albion Rovers (Parkhead) 4–1
Final
v Partick Thistle (Parkhead) 0–1

1921–22
Round 1
v Clachnacuddin (a) 5–0
Round 2
v Albion Rovers (a) 1–1
Replay
v Albion Rovers (h) 4–0
Round 3
v Heart of Midlothian (a) 4–0
Round 4
v St Mirren (h) 1–1
Replay
v St Mirren (a) 2–0
Semi-final
v Partick Thistle (h) 2–0

Final
v Morton (H) 0–1

1922–23
Round 1
v Clyde (a) 4–0
Round 2
v Ayr United (a) 0–2

1923–24
Round 1
v Lochgelly United (h) 4–1
Round 2
v St Mirren (a) 1–0
Round 3
v Hibernian (h) 1–2

1924–25
Round 1
v East Fife (a) 3–1
Round 2
v Montrose (a) 2–0
Round 3
v Arbroath (h) 5–3
Round 4
v Kilmarnock (a) 2–1
Semi-final
v Celtic (H) 0–5

1925–26
Round 1
v Lochgelly United (h) 3–0
Round 2
v Stenhousemuir (h) 1–0
Round 3
v Falkirk (a) 2–0
Round 4
v Morton (a) 4–0
Semi-final
v St Mirren (Parkhead) 0–1

1926–27
Round 1
v Leith Athletic (a) 4–1
Round 2
v St Mirren (h) 6–0
Round 3
v Hamilton Acas. (h) 4–0
Round 4
v Falkirk (a) 2–2
Replay*
v Falkirk (h) 0–1
* After extra time

1927–28
Round 1
v East Stirlingshire (a) 6–0
Round 2
v Cowdenbeath (h) 4–2
Round 3
v King's Park (h) 3–1
Round 4
v Albion Rovers (a) 1–0
Semi-final
v Hibernian (Tynecastle) 3–0

Final
v Celtic (H) 4–0

1928–29
Round 1
v Edinburgh City (h) 11–1
Round 2
v Partick Thistle (h) 5–1
Round 3
v Clyde (a) 2–0
Round 4
v Dundee United (h) 3–1
Semi-final
v St Mirren (H) 3–2
Final
v Kilmarnock (H) 0–2

1929–30
Round 1
v Queen's Park (a) 1–0
Round 2
v Cowdenbeath (h) 2–2
Replay
v Cowdenbeath (a) 3–0
Round 3
v Motherwell (a) 5–2
Round 4
v Montrose (h) 3–0
Semi-final
v Heart of Midlothian (H) 4–1
Final
v Partick Thistle (H) 0–0
Replay
v Partick Thistle (H) 2–1

1930–31
Round 1
v Armadale (a) 7–1
Round 2
v Dundee (h) 1–2

1931–32
Round 1
v Brechin City (h) 8–2
Round 2
v Raith Rovers (a) 5–0
Round 3
v Heart of Midlothian (a) 1–0
Round 4
v Motherwell (h) 2–0
Semi-final
v Hamilton Acas. (Parkhead) 5–2
Final
v Kilmarnock (H) 1–1
Replay
v Kilmarnock (H) 3–0

1932–33
Round 1
v Arbroath (h) 3–1

Round 2
v Queen's Park (h) 1–1
Replay
v Queen's Park (a) 1–1
Replay
v Queen's Park (a) 3–1
Round 3
v Kilmarnock (a) 0–1

1933–34
Round 1
v Blairgowrie (h) 14–2
Round 2
v Third Lanark (a) 3–0
Round 3
v Heart of Midlothian (h) 0–0
Replay
v Heart of Midlothian (a) 2–1
Round 4
v Aberdeen (h) 1–0
Semi-final
v St Johnstone (H) 1–0
Final
v St Mirren (H) 5–0

1934–35
Round 1
v Cowdenbeath (h) 3–1
Round 2
v Third Lanark (h) 2–0
Round 3
v St Mirren (h) 1–0
Round 4
v Motherwell (a) 4–1
Semi-final
v Heart of Midlothian (H) 1–1
Replay
v Heart of Midlothian (H) 2–0
Final
v Hamilton Acas. (H) 2–1

1935–36
Round 1
v East Fife (h) 3–1
Round 2
v Albion Rovers (a) 3–1
Round 3
v St Mirren (a) 2–1
Round 4
v Aberdeen (a) 1–0
Semi-final
v Clyde (H) 3–0
Final
v Third Lanark (H) 1–0

1936–37
Round 1
v Queen of the South (a) 0–1

1937–38
Round 1
v Alloa (a) 6–1
Round 2
v Queen of the South (h) 3–1
Round 3
A Bye
Round 4
v Falkirk (a) 2–1
Semi-final
v Kilmarnock (H) 3–4

1938–39
Round 1
v Raith Rovers (a) 1–0
Round 2
v Hamilton Acas. (h) 2–0
Round 3
v Clyde (h) 1–4

1946–47
Round 1
v Clyde (h) 2–1
Round 2
v Hibernian (h) 0–0
Replay
v Hibernian (a) 0–2

1947–48
Round 1
v Stranraer (a) 1–0
Round 2
v Leith Athletic (h) 4–0
Round 3
v Partick Thistle (h) 3–0
Round 4
v East Fife (h) 1–0
Semi-final
v Hibernian (H) 1–0
Final*
v Morton (H) 1–1
Replay*
v Morton (H) 1–0
* After extra time

1948–49
Round 1
v Elgin City (h) 6–1
Round 2
v Motherwell (a) 3–0
Round 3
A Bye
Round 4
v Partick Thistle (h) 4–0
Semi-final
v East Fife (H) 3–0
Final
v Clyde (H) 4–1

1949–50
Round 1
v Motherwell (a) 4–2

Round 2
v Cowdenbeath (h) 8–0
Round 3
A Bye
Round 4
v Raith Rovers (h) 1–1
*Replay**
v Raith Rovers (a) 1–1
Replay
v Raith Rovers (h) 2–0
Semi-final
v Queen of the South (H) 1–1
Replay
v Queen of the South (H) 3–0
Final
v East Fife (H) 3–0
* After extra time

1950–51
Round 1
v Queen of the South (h) 2–0
Round 2
v Hibernian (h) 2–3

1951–52
Round 2
v Elgin City (h) 6–1
Round 3
v Arbroath (a) 2–0
Round 4
v Motherwell (h) 1–1
Replay
v Motherwell (a) 1–2

1952–53
Round 1
v Arbroath (h) 4–0
Round 2
v Dundee (a) 2–0
Round 3
v Morton (a) 4–1
Round 4
v Celtic (h) 2–0
Semi-final
v Hearts (H) 2–1
Final
v Aberdeen (H) 1–1
Replay
v Aberdeen (H) 1–0

1953–54
Round 1
v Queen's Park (h) 2–0
Round 2
v Kilmarnock (h) 2–2
Replay
v Kilmarnock (a) 3–1
Round 3
v Third Lanark (a) 0–0
*Replay**
v Third Lanark (h) 4–4

Replay
v Third Lanark (h) 3–2
Round 4
v Berwick Rangers (h) 4–0
Semi-final
v Aberdeen (H) 0–6
* After extra time

1954–55
Round 5
v Dundee (h) 0–0
Replay
v Dundee (a) 1–0
Round 6
v Aberdeen (a) 1–2

1955–56
Round 5
v Aberdeen (h) 2–1
Round 6
v Dundee (a) 1–0
Round 7
v Hearts (a) 0–4

1956–57
Round 5
v Hearts (a) 4–0
Round 6
v Celtic (a) 4–4
Replay
v Celtic (h) 0–2

1957–58
Round 1
v Cowdenbeath (a) 3–1
Round 2
v Forfar Athletic (a) 9–1
Round 3
v Dunfermline Ath. (a) 2–1
Round 4
v Queen of the South (a) 4–3
Semi-final
v Hibernian (H) 2–2
Replay
v Hibernian (H) 1–2

1958–59
Round 1
v Forfar Athletic (a) 3–1
Round 2
v Hearts (h) 3–2
Round 3
v Celtic (a) 1–2

1959–60
Round 1
v Berwick Rangers (a) 3–1
Round 2
v Arbroath (h) 2–0
Round 3
v Stenhousemuir (a) 3–0
Round 4
v Hibernian (h) 3–2

Semi-final
v Celtic (H) 1–1
Replay
v Celtic (H) 4–1
Final
v Kilmarnock (H) 2–0

1960–61
Round 2
v Dundee (a) 5–1
Round 3
v Motherwell (a) 2–2
Replay
v Motherwell (h) 2–5

1961–62
Round 1
v Falkirk (a) 2–1
Round 2
v Arbroath (h) 6–0
Round 3
v Aberdeen (a) 2–2
Replay
v Aberdeen (h) 5–1
Round 4
v Kilmarnock (a) 4–2
Semi-final
v Motherwell (H) 3–1
Final
v St Mirren (H) 2–0

1962–63
Round 2
v Airdrieonians (a) 6–0
Round 3
v East Stirlingshire (h) 7–2
Round 4
v Dundee (a) 1–1
Replay
v Dundee (h) 3–2
Semi-final
v Dundee United (H) 5–2
Final
v Celtic (H) 1–1
Replay
v Celtic (H) 3–0

1963–64
Round 1
v Stenhousemuir (a) 5–1
Round 2
v Duns (h) 9–0
Round 3
v Partick Thistle (h) 3–0
Round 4
v Celtic (h) 2–0
Semi-final
v Dunfermline Ath. (H) 1–0
Final
v Dundee (H) 3–1

1964–65
Round 1
v Hamilton Acas. (h) 3–0
Round 2
v Dundee United (a) 2–0
Round 3
v Hibernian (a) 1–2

1965–66
Round 1
v Airdrieonians (h) 5–1
Round 2
v Ross County (a) 2–0
Round 3
v St Johnstone (h) 1–0
Semi-final
v Aberdeen (H) 0–0
Replay
v Aberdeen (H) 2–1
Final
v Celtic (H) 0–0
Replay
v Celtic (H) 1–0

1966–67
Round 1
v Berwick Rangers (a) 0–1

1967–68
Round 1
v Hamilton Acas. (h) 3–1
Round 2
v Dundee (a) 1–1
Replay
v Dundee (h) 4–1
Round 3
v Hearts (h) 1–1
Replay
v Hearts (a) 0–1

1968–69
Round 1
v Hibernian (h) 1–0
Round 2
v Hearts (h) 2–0
Round 3
v Airdrieonians (h) 1–0
Semi-final
v Aberdeen (Parkhead) 6–1
Final
v Celtic (H) 0–4

1969–70
Round 1
v Hibernian (h) 3–1
Round 2
v Forfar Athletic (a) 7–0
Round 3
v Celtic (a) 1–3

1970–71
Round 3
v Falkirk (h) 3–0

Round 4
v St Mirren (a) 3–1
Round 5
v Aberdeen (h) 1–0
Semi-final
v Hibernian (H) 0–0
Replay
v Hibernian (H) 2–1
Final
v Celtic (H) 1–1
Replay
v Celtic (H) 1–2

1971–72
Round 3
v Falkirk (a) 2–2
Replay
v Falkirk (h) 2–0
Round 4
v St Mirren (a) 4–1
Round 5
v Motherwell (a) 2–2
Replay
v Motherwell (h) 4–2
Semi-final
v Hibernian (H) 1–1
Replay
v Hibernian (H) 0–2

1972–73
Round 3
v Dundee United (h) 1–0
Round 4
v Hibernian (h) 1–1
Replay
v Hibernian (a) 2–1
Round 5
v Airdrieonians (h) 2–0
Semi-final
v Ayr United (H) 2–0
Final
v Celtic (H) 3–2

1973–74
Round 3
v Queen's Park (h) 8–0
Round 4
v Dundee (h) 0–3

1974–75
Round 3
v Aberdeen (a) 1–1
Replay
v Aberdeen (h) 1–2

1975–76
Round 3
v East Fife (h) 3–0
Round 4
v Aberdeen (h) 4–1
Round 5
v Queen of the South (a) 5–0
Semi-final
v Motherwell (H) 3–2

Final
v Hearts (H) 3–1

1976–77
Round 3
v Falkirk (h) 3–1
Round 4
v Elgin City (h) 3–0
Round 5
v Motherwell (h) 2–0
Semi-final
v Hearts (H) 2–0
Final
v Celtic (H) 0–1

1977–78
Round 3
v Berwick Rangers (a) 4–2
Round 4
v Stirling Albion (h) 1–0
Round 5
v Kilmarnock (h) 4–1
Semi-final
v Dundee United (H) 2–0
Final
v Aberdeen (H) 2–1

1978–79
Round 3
v Motherwell (h) 3–1
Round 4
v Kilmarnock (h) 1–1
Replay
v Kilmarnock (a) 1–0
Round 5
v Dundee (h) 6–3
Semi-final
v Partick Thistle (H) 0–0
Replay
v Partick Thistle (H) 1–0
Final
v Hibernian (H) 0–0
Replay
v Hibernian (H) 0–0
Second Replay
v Hibernian (H) 3–2

1979–80
Round 3
v Clyde (a) 2–2
Replay
v Clyde (h) 2–0
Round 4
v Dundee United (h) 1–0
Round 5
v Hearts (h) 6–1
Semi-final
v Aberdeen (Parkhead) 1–0
Final
v Celtic (H) 0–1

1980–81
Round 3
v Airdrieonians (a) 5–0
Round 4
v St Johnstone (a) 3–3
Replay
v St Johnstone (h) 3–1
Round 5
v Hibernian (h) 3–1
Semi-final
v Morton (H) 2–1
Final
v Dundee United (H) 0–0
Replay
v Dundee United (H) 4–1

1981–82
Round 3
v Albion Rovers (h) 6–2
Round 4
v Dumbarton (h) 4–0
Round 5
v Dundee (h) 2–0
Semi-final
v Forfar Athletic (H) 0–0
Replay
v Forfar Athletic (H) 3–1
Final
v Aberdeen (H) 1–4*
* After extra time

1982–83
Round 3
v Falkirk (a) 2–0
Round 4
v Forfar Athletic (h) 2–1
Round 5
v Queen's Park (a) 2–1
Semi-final
v St Mirren (Parkhead) 1–1
Replay
v St Mirren (H) 1–0
Final
v Aberdeen (H) 0–1

1983–84
Round 3
v Dunfermline (h) 2–1
Round 4
v Inverness Caley (a) 6–0
Round 5
v Dundee (a) 2–2
Replay
v Dundee (h) 2–3

1984–85
Round 3
v Morton (a) 3–3
Replay
v Morton (h) 3–1
Round 4
v Dundee (h) 0–1

1985–86
Round 3
v Hearts (a) 2–3

1986–87
Round 3
v Hamilton Acas. (h) 0–1

1987–88
Round 3
v Raith Rovers (a) 0–0
Replay
v Raith Rovers (h) 4–1
Round 4
v Dumfermline (a) 0–2

1988–89
Round 3
v Raith Rovers (a) 1–1
Replay
v Raith Rovers (h) 3–0
Round 4
v Stranraer (h) 8–0
Round 5
v Dundee United (h) 2–2
Replay
v Dundee United (a) 1–0
Semi-final
v St Johnstone (Parkhead) 0–0
Replay
v St Johnstone (Parkhead) 4–0
Final
v Celtic (H) 0–1

SCOTTISH LEAGUE CUP

1946–47
v St Mirren (h) 4–0
v St Mirren (a) 4–0
v Queen's Park (h) 1–0
v Queen's Park (a) 4–2
v Morton (h) 3–0
v Morton (a) 2–0
Quarter-final
v Dundee United (h) 2–1
v Dundee United (a) 1–1
Semi-final
v Hibernian (H) 3–1
Final
v Aberdeen (H) 4–0

1947–48
v Celtic (h) 2–0
v Celtic (a) 0–2
v Dundee (h) 3–0
v Dundee (a) 1–1
v Third Lanark (h) 3–0
v Third Lanark (a) 3–1

Quarter-final
v Stenhousemuir (h) 2–0
Semi-final
v Falkirk (H) 0–1

1948–49
v Celtic (h) 2–1
v Celtic (a) 1–3
v Clyde (h) 1–1
v Clyde (a) 3–1
v Hibernian (h) 1–0
v Hibernian (a) 0–0
Quarter-final
v St Mirren (h) 1–0
Semi-final
v Dundee (H) 4–1
Final
v Raith Rovers (H) 2–0

1949–50
v Aberdeen (h) 4–2
v Aberdeen (a) 1–1
v Celtic (h) 2–0
v Celtic (a) 2–3
v St Mirren (h) 5–1
v St Mirren (a) 1–1
Quarter-final
v Cowdenbeath (h) 2–3
v Cowdenbeath (a) 3–1*
Semi-final
v East Fife (H) 1–2*
* After extra time

1950–51
v Aberdeen (h) 1–2
v Aberdeen (a) 0–2
v Clyde (h) 4–0
v Clyde (a) 5–1
v Morton (h) 6–1
v Morton (a) 2–1

1951–52
v Aberdeen (h) 2–1
v Aberdeen (a) 1–2
v East Fife (a) 0–0
v East Fife (h) 4–1
v Queen of the South (a) 3–0
v Queen of the South (h) 5–2
Quarter-final
v Dunfermline (a) 0–1
v Dunfermline (h) 3–1
Semi-final
v Celtic (H) 3–0
Final
v Dundee (H) 2–3

1952–53
v Hearts (a) 0–5
v Hearts (h) 2–0
v Motherwell (h) 2–0
v Motherwell (a) 3–3
v Aberdeen (h) 3–1
v Aberdeen (a) 2–1

Quarter-final
v Third Lanark (h) 0–0
v Third Lanark (a) 2–0
Semi-final
v Kilmarnock (H) 0–1

1953–54
v Raith Rovers (a) 4–0
v Raith Rovers (h) 3–1
v Hamilton Acad. (h) 5–1
v Hamilton Acad. (a) 5–0
v Hearts (h) 4–1
v Hearts (a) 1–1
Quarter-final
v Ayr United (h) 4–2
v Ayr United (a) 2–3
Semi-final
v Partick Thistle (H) 0–2

1954–55
v Partick Thistle (h) 1–1
v Partick Thistle (a) 1–2
v Clyde (h) 1–3
v Clyde (a) 2–1
v Stirling Albion (a) 5–0
v Stirling Albion (h) 2–0
Quarter-final
v Motherwell (a) 1–2
v Motherwell (h) 1–1

1955–56
v Falkirk (a) 5–0
v Falkirk (h) 4–3
v Queen of the South (a) 2–1
v Queen of the South (h) 6–0
v Celtic (h) 1–4
v Celtic (a) 4–0
Quarter-final
v Hamilton 2–1
v Hamilton (h) 8–0
Semi-final
v Aberdeen (H) 1–2

1956–57
v Celtic (a) 1–2
v Celtic (h) 0–0
v Aberdeen (a) 6–2
v Aberdeen (h) 4–1
v East Fife (a) 4–1
v East Fife (h) 3–0

1957–58
v St Mirren (h) 6–0
v St Mirren (a) 4–0
v Partick Thistle (h) 0–3
v Partick Thistle (a) 1–0
v Raith Rovers (h) 4–3
v Raith Rovers (a) 3–4
Quarter-final
v Kilmarnock (a) 2–1
v Kilmarnock (h) 3–1
Semi-final
v Brechin City (H) 4–0

Final
v Celtic (H) 1–7

1958–59
v Hearts (h) 3–0
v Hearts (a) 1–2
v Raith Rovers (h) 6–0
v Raith Rovers (a) 1–3
v Third Lanark (h) 2–2
v Third Lanark (a) 3–0

1959–60
v Hibernian (a) 6–1
v Hibernian (h) 5–1
v Motherwell (h) 1–2
v Motherwell (h) 1–2
v Dundee (h) 2–0
v Dundee (a) 3–2

1960–61
v Partick Thistle (h) 3–1
v Partick Thistle (a) 4–1
v Third Lanark (h) 3–2
v Third Lanark (a) 1–2
v Celtic (h) 2–3
v Celtic (a) 2–1
Quarter-final
v Dundee (h) 1–0
v Dundee (a) 4–3
Semi-final
v Queen of the South (Parkhead) 7–0
Final
v Kilmarnock (H) 2–0

1961–62
v Third Lanark (h) 5–0
v Third Lanark (a) 2–0
v Dundee (h) 4–2
v Dundee (a) 1–1
v Airdrieonians (h) 4–1
v Airdrieonians (a) 2–1
Quarter-final
v East Fife (h) 3–1
v East Fife (a) 3–1
Semi-final
v St Johnstone (Parkhead) 3–2
After extra time
Final
v Hearts (H) 1–1
After extra time
Replay
v Hearts (H) 3–1

1962–63
v Hibernian (a) 4–1
v Hibernian (h) 0–0
v Third Lanark (h) 5–2
v Third Lanark (a) 5–2
v St Mirren (a) 1–2
v St Mirren (h) 4–0

Quarter-final
v Dumbarton (a) 3–1
v Dumbarton (h) 1–1
Semi-final
v Kilmarnock (H) 2–3

1963–64
v Celtic (a) 3–0
v Celtic (h) 3–0
v Queen of the South (h) 5–2
v Queen of the South (a) 5–2
v Kilmarnock (h) 2–2
v Kilmarnock (a) 4–1
Quarter-final
v East Fife (a) 1–1
v East Fife (h) 2–0
Semi-final
v Berwick Rangers (H) 3–1
Final
v Morton (H) 5–0

1964–65
v Aberdeen (h) 4–0
v Aberdeen (a) 4–3
v St Mirren (a) 0–0
v St Mirren (h) 6–2
v St Johnstone (a) 9–1
v St Johnstone (h) 3–1
Quarter-final
v Dunfermline (a) 3–0
v Dunfermline (h) 2–2
Semi-final
v Dundee United (H) 2–1
After extra time
Final
v Celtic (H) 2–1

1965–66
v Aberdeen (a) 0–2
v Aberdeen (h) 4–0
v Hearts (a) 2–4
v Hearts (h) 1–0
v Clyde (h) 3–0
v Clyde (a) 3–1
Quarter-final
v Airdrieonians (a) 5–1
v Airdrieonians (h) 4–0
Semi-final
v Kilmarnock (H) 6–4
Final
v Celtic (H) 1–2

1966–67
v Hibernian (h) 1–0
v Stirling Albion (a) 8–0
v Kilmarnock (h) 0–0
v Hibernian (a) 2–3
v Stirling Albion (h) 1–1
v Kilmarnock (a) 1–0
Quarter-final
v Ayr United (a) 1–1
v Ayr United (h) 3–0

Semi-final
v Aberdeen (H) 2–2
Replay
v Aberdeen (H) 2–0
Final
v Celtic (H) 0–1

1967–68
v Aberdeen (a) 1–1
v Celtic (h) 1–1
v Dundee United (h) 1–0
v Aberdeen (h) 3–0
v Celtic (a) 1–3
v Dundee United (a) 3–0

1968–69
v Celtic (h) 0–2
v Partick Thistle (a) 5–1
v Morton (h) 2–0
v Celtic (a) 0–1
v Partick Thistle (h) 2–1
v Morton (a) 5–0

1969–70
v Raith Rovers (a) 3–2
v Celtic (h) 2–1
v Airdrieonians (a) 3–0
v Celtic (a) 0–1
v Raith Rovers (h) 3–3
v Airdrieonians (h) 3–0

1970–71
v Dunfermline (h) 4–1
v Motherwell (a) 2–0
v Morton (h) 0–0
v Motherwell (h) 2–0
v Dunfermline (a) 6–0
v Morton (a) 2–0
Quarter-final
v Hibernian (h) 3–1
v Hibernian (a) 3–1
Semi-final
v Cowdenbeath (H) 2–0
Final
v Celtic (H) 1–0

1971–72
v Celtic (a) 0–2
v Ayr United (h) 4–0
v Morton (h) 2–0
v Ayr United (a) 4–0
v Celtic (h) 0–3
v Morton (a) 1–0

1972–73
v Clydebank (h) 2–0
v St Mirren (a) 4–0
v Ayr United (h) 2–1
v St Mirren (h) 1–4
v Clydebank (a) 5–0
v Ayr United (a) 2–1
Round 2
v Stenhuismuir (a) 5–0
v Stenhuismuir (h) 1–2

Quarter-final
v St Johnstone (h) 1–1
v St Johnstone (a) 2–0
Semi-final
v Hibernian (H) 0–1

1973–74
v Falkirk (h) 3–1
v Arbroath (a) 2–1
v Celtic (h) 1–2
v Arbroath (h) 3–0
v Celtic (a) 3–1
v Falkirk (a) 5–1
Round 2
v Dumbarton (h) 6–0
v Dumbarton (a) 2–1
Quarter-final
v Hibernian (h) 2–0
v Hibernian (a) 0–0
Semi-final
v Celtic (H) 1–3

1974–75
v St Johnstone (h) 3–2
v Hibernian (a) 1–3
v St Johnstone (a) 6–3
v Dundee (a) 2–0
v Dundee (h) 4–0
v Hibernian (h) 0–1

1975–76
v Airdrie (h) 6–1
v Clyde (a) 1–0
v Motherwell (h) 1–1
v Clyde (h) 6–0
v Motherwell (a) 2–2
v Airdrie (a) 2–1
Quarter-final
v Queen of the South (h) 1–0
v Queen of the South (a) 2–2
Semi-final
v Montrose (H) 5–1
Final
v Celtic (H) 1–0

1976–77
v St Johnstone (h) 5–0
v Hibernian (a) 1–1
v Montrose (h) 4–0
v Hibernian (h) 3–0
v Montrose (a) 3–0
v St Johnstone (a) 1–0
Quarter-final
v Clydebank (h) 3–3
v Clydebank (a) 1–1
Play-off 1
v Clydebank (h) 0–0
Play-off 2
v Clydebank (Firhill) 2–1
Semi-final
v Aberdeen (H) 1–5

1977–78
Round 2
v St Johnstone (h) 3–1
v St Johnstone (a) 3–0
Round 3
v Aberdeen (h) 6–1
v Aberdeen (a) 1–3
Quarter-final
v Dunfermline (h) 3–1
v Dunfermline (a) 3–1
Semi-final
v Forfar Athletic (H) 5–2
Final
v Celtic (H) 2–1

1978–79
Round 1
v Albion Rovers (h) 3–0
v Albion Rovers (a) 1–0
Round 2
v Forfar Athletic (h) 3–0
v Forfar Athletic (a) 4–1
Round 3
v St Mirren (h) 3–2
v St Mirren (a) 0–0
Quarter-final
v Arbroath (h) 1–0
v Arbroath (a) 2–1
Semi-final
v Celtic (H) 3–2
Final
v Aberdeen (H) 2–1

1979–80
Round 2
v Clyde (a) 2–1
v Clyde (h) 4–0
Round 3
v Aberdeen (a) 1–3
v Aberdeen (h) 0–2

1980–81
Round 1
v Forfar Athletic (a) 2–0
v Forfar Athletic (h) 3–1
Round 2
v Aberdeen (h) 1–0
v Aberdeen (a) 1–3

1981–82
v Morton (a) 1–1
v Dundee (h) 4–1
v Raith Rovers (h) 8–1
v Dundee (a) 2–1
v Morton (h) 1–0
v Raith Rovers (a) 3–1
Quarter-final
v Brechin City (a) 4–0
v Brechin City (h) 1–0
Semi-final
v St Mirren (a) 2–2
v St Mirren (h) 2–1

Final
v Dundee United (H) 2–1

1982–83
v Hibernian (a) 1–1
v Airdrie (h) 3–1
v Clydebank (a) 4–1
v Airdrie (a) 2–1
v Hibernian (h) 0–0
v Clydebank (h) 3–2
Quarter-final
v Kilmarnock (a) 6–1
v Kilmarnock (h) 6–0
Semi-final
v Hearts (h) 2–0
v Hearts (a) 2–1
Final
v Celtic (H) 1–2

1983–84
Round 2
v Queen of the South (h) 4–0
v Queen of the South (a) 4–1
Round 3 (Section)
v Clydebank (h) 4–0
v Hearts (a) 3–0
v St Mirren (h) 5–0
v Hearts (h) 2–0
v Clydebank (a) 3–0
v St Mirren (a) 1–0
Semi-final
v Dundee United (a) 1–1
v Dundee United (h) 2–0
Final
v Celtic (H) 3–2

1984–85
Round 2
v Falkirk (h) 1–0
Round 3
v Raith Rovers (h) 4–0
Quarter-final
v Cowdenbeath (a) 3–1
Semi-final
v Meadowbank Thistle (h)
4–0
v Meadowbank Thistle (a)
1–1
Final
v Dundee United (H) 1–0

1985–86
Round 2
v Clyde (h) 5–0
Round 3
v Forfar Athletic (a) 2–2
Rangers won 6–5 on penalties
Quarter-final
v Hamilton Acads (a) 2–1
Semi-final
v Hibernian (a) 0–2
v Hibernian (h) 1–0

1986–87
Round 2
v Stenhousemuir (a) 4–1
Round 3
v East Fife (a) 0–0
Rangers won 5–4 on penalties
Quarter-final
v Dundee (h) 3–1
Semi-final
v Dundee United (H) 2–1
Final
v Celtic (H) 2–1

1987–88
Round 2
v Stirling Albion (a) 2–1
Round 3
v Dunfermline (a) 4–1
Quarter-final
v Hearts (h) 4–1
Semi-final
v Motherwell (H) 3–1
Final
v Aberdeen (H) 3–3
Rangers won 5–3 on penalties

1988–89
Round 2
v Clyde (a) 3–0
Round 3
v Clydebank (h) 6–0
Quarter-final
v Dundee (h) 4–1
Semi-final
v Hearts (H) 3–0
Final
v Aberdeen (H) 3–2

RANGERS IN EUROPE

EUROPEAN CUP
1956–57
Round 2 1st leg
v Nice (h) 2–1
Round 2 2nd leg
v Nice (a) 1–2
Play-off
v Nice (Paris) 1–3

1957–58
Round 1 1st leg
v St Etienne (h) 3–1
Round 1 2nd leg
v St Etienne (a) 1–2
Round 2 1st leg
v AC Milan (h) 1–4

Round 2 2nd leg
v AC Milan (a) 0–2

1959–60
Round 1 1st leg
v Anderlecht (h) 5–2
Round 1 2nd leg
v Anderlecht (a) 2–0
Round 2 1st leg
v Red Star Bratislava (h) 4–3
Round 2 2nd leg
v Red Star Bratislava (a) 1–1
Quarter-final 1st leg
v Sparta (Rotterdam) (a) 3–2
Quarter-final 2nd leg
v Sparta (h) 0–1
Play-off
v Sparta (Highbury) 3–2
Semi-final 1st leg
v Eintracht Frankfurt (a) 1–6
Semi-final 2nd leg
v Eintracht Frankfurt (h) 3–6

1961–62
Round 1 1st leg
v Monaco (a) 3–2
Round 1 2nd leg
v Monaco (h) 3–2
Round 2 1st leg
v Vorwaerts (E. Germany) (a)
2–1
Round 2 2nd leg
v Vorwaerts (h) 4–1*
Quarter-final 1st leg
v Standard Liege (a) 1–4
Quarter-final 2nd leg
v Standard Liege (h) 2–0
* Played in Sweden

1963–64
Round 1 1st leg
v Real Madrid (h) 0–1
Round 1 2nd leg
v Real Madrid (a) 0–6

1964–65
Round 1 1st leg
v Red Star Belgrade (h) 3–1
Round 1 2nd leg
v Red Star Belgrade (a) 2–4
Play-off
v Red Star Belgrade (Highbury) 3–1
Round 2 1st leg
v Sportklub Rapid (Austria)
(h) 1–0
Round 2 2nd leg
v Sportklub Rapid (a) 2–0
Quarter-final 1st leg
v Inter Milan (a) 1–3
Quarter-final 2nd leg
v Inter Milan (h) 1–0

1975–76
Round 1 1st leg
v Bohemians (h) 4–1
Round 1 2nd leg
v Bohemians (a) 1–1
Round 2 1st leg
v St Etienne (a) 0–2
Round 2 2nd leg
v St Etienne (h) 1–2

1976–77
Round 1 1st leg
v FC Zurich (h) 1–1
Round 1 2nd leg
v FC Zurich (a) 0–1

1978–79
Round 1 1st leg
v Juventus (a) 0–1
Round 1 2nd leg
v Juventus (h) 2–0
Round 2 1st leg
v PSV Eindhoven (h) 0–0
Round 2 2nd leg
v PSV Eindhoven (a) 3–2
Quarter-final 1st leg
v Cologne (a) 0–1
Quarter-final 2nd leg
v Cologne (h) 1–1

1987–88
Round 1 1st leg
v Dynamo Kiev (a) 0–1
Round 1 2nd leg
v Dynamo Kiev (h) 2–0
Round 2 1st leg
v Gornik Zabrze (h) 3–1
Round 2 2nd leg
v Gornik Zabrze (a) 1–1
Quarter-final 1st leg
v Steaua Bucharest (a) 0–2
Quarter-final 2nd leg
v Steaua Bucharest (h) 2–1

EUROPEAN CUP-WINNERS' CUP

1960–61
Round 1 1st leg
v Ferencvaros (h) 4–2
Round 1 2nd leg
v Ferencvaros (a) 1–2
Round 2 1st leg
v Borussia Moenchen-gladbach (a) 3–0
Round 2 2nd leg
v Borussia (h) 8–0
Semi-final 1st leg
v Wolverhampton W. (h) 2–0

Semi-final 2nd leg
v Wolverhampton W. (a) 1–1
Final 1st leg
v Fiorentina (h) 0–2
Final 2nd leg
v Fiorentina (a) 1–2

1962–63
Round 1 1st leg
v Seville (h) 4–0
Round 1 2nd leg
v Seville (a) 0–2
Round 2 1st leg
v Tottenham H. (a) 2–5
Round 2 2nd leg
v Tottenham H. (h) 2–3

1966–67
Round 1 1st leg
v Glentoran (a) 1–1
Round 1 2nd leg
v Glentoran (h) 4–0
Round 2 1st leg
v Borussia Dortmund (h) 2–1
Round 2 2nd leg
v Borussia Dortmund (a) 0–0
Quarter-final 1st leg
v Saragossa (h) 2–0
Quarter-final 2nd leg
v Saragossa (a) 0–2
Rangers won toss-up
Semi-final 1st leg
v Slavia Sofia (a) 1–0
Semi-final 2nd leg
v Slavia Sofia (h) 1–0
Final
v Bayern Munich (Nuremburg) 0–1
After extra time

1969–70
Round 1 1st leg
v Steaua Bucharest (h) 2–0
Round 2 2nd leg
v Steaua Bucharest (a) 0–0
Round 2 1st leg
v Gornik (a) 1–3
Round 2 2nd leg
v Gornik (h) 1–3

1971–72
Round 1 1st leg
v Rennes (a) 1–1
Round 1 2nd leg
v Rennes (h) 1–0
Round 2 1st leg
v Sporting Lisbon (h) 3–2
Round 2 2nd leg
v Sporting Lisbon (a) 3–4
Rangers won on away goals rule

Round 3 1st leg
v Torino (a) 1–1
Round 3 2nd leg
v Torino (h) 1–0
Semi-final 1st leg
v Bayern Munich (a) 1–1
Semi-final 2nd leg
v Bayern Munich (h) 2–0
Final
v Moscow Dynamo (Barcelona) 3–2

1973–74
Round 1 1st leg
v Ankaragucu (a) 2–0
Round 2 2nd leg
v Ankaragucu (h) 4–0
Round 2 1st leg
v Borussia MG (a) 0–3
Round 2 2nd leg
v Borussia MG (h) 3–2

1977–78
Preliminary Round 1st leg
v Young Boys (h) 1–0
Preliminary Round 2nd leg
v Young Boys (a) 2–2
Round 1 1st leg
v Twente Enschede (h) 0–0
Round 1 2nd leg
v Twente Enschede (a) 0–3

1979–80
Preliminary Round 1st leg
v Lillestrom (h) 1–0
Preliminary Round 2nd leg
v Lillestrom (a) 2–0
Round 1 1st leg
v Fortuna Dusseld'f (h) 2–1
Round 1 2nd leg
v Fortuna Dusseld'f (a) 0–0
Round 2 1st leg
v Valencia (a) 1–1
Round 2 2nd leg
v Valencia (h) 1–3

1981–82
Round 1 1st leg
v Dukla Prague (a) 0–3
Round 2 2nd leg
v Dukla Prague (h) 2–1

1983–84
Round 1 1st leg
v Valetta (a) 8–0
Round 1 2nd leg
v Valetta (h) 10–0
Round 2 1st leg
v Porto (h) 2–1
Round 2 2nd leg
v Porto 0–1
Porto won on away goals